SYMBOLIC COMPUTATION

Managing Editors: J. Encarnaçao P. Hayes

Artificial Intelligence
Editors: L. Bolc A. Bundy J. Siekmann

The Design of Interpreters, Compilers, and Editors for Augmented Transition Networks

Edited by Leonard Bolc

With 72 Figures

Springer-Verlag
Berlin Heidelberg New York Tokyo 1983

Leonard Bolc

Institute of Informatics, Warsaw University
PKiN, pok. 850, 00-901 Warszawa, Poland

ISBN 3-540-12789-5 Springer-Verlag Berlin Heidelberg New York Tokyo
ISBN 0-387-12789-5 Springer-Verlag New York Heidelberg Berlin Tokyo

© Springer-Verlag Berlin Heidelberg 1983
Printed in Germany

Printing: Beltz Offsetdruck, Hemsbach/Bergstr.; Bookbinding: J. Schäffer OHG, Grünstadt
2145/3140-543210

KH
7-1-84

Preface

Augmented Transition Network Grammars are at present the most widely
used method for analyzing natural languages. Despite the increasing po-
pularity of this method, however, no extensive papers on ATN-Grammars
have been presented which would be accessible to a larger number of per-
sons engaged in the problem from both the theoretical and practical
points of view.

Augmented Transition Networks (ATN) are derived from state automata.
Like a finite state automaton, an ATN consists of a collection of labeled states and arcs, a distinguished start state and a set of distinguished final states. States are connected with each other by arcs creating a directed graph or net. The label on an arc indicates a terminal
symbol (word) or the type of words which must occur in an input stream
to allow the transition to the next state. It is said that a sequence
of words (or sentence) is accepted by such a net if there exists a sequence of arcs (usually called a path), connecting the start state with
a final state, which can be followed to the sentence.

The finite state automaton is then enriched by several facilities which
increase its computational power. The most important of them permits
some arcs to be labeled by nonterminal rather than terminal symbols.
This means that the transition through such an arc is actually the recursive application of the net beginning with a pointed state.

The simple consequence of this is a partition of the net into a collection of independent specialized subnets which can accept definite types
of sentences. The facility is assured by a pair of PUSH and POP arcs.
The transition through the PUSH arc causes the current computation to
be suspended and a new process established with a start state indicated
by the arc parameter. The "pseudo" arc POP leaves a state but has no
destination. The POP arc may be placed only in the final state of a subnet and causes the lower level computation called by a previous PUSH arc
to be closed and the higher level reactivated at the same point where
is had been suspended. The PUSH/POP facility assures the recognition of
entire sentence constituents.

Such a network is formally equivalent to a pushdown store automaton and can accept context-free languages. We call it a basic transition network (BTN) [Woods, 1972]. Apart from PUSH and POP arcs a BTN also has three other types of arcs. A WRD arc allows the transition with a terminal symbol (word). A CAT arc may be traversed when an indicated type of word is recognized in the input sequence. A JUMP arc allows the transition without any examination of the input. This arc does not cause the input pointer to move.

To make the model more powerful each arc is then equipped with a test and a sequence of actions. The test is an arbitrary condition which must be satisfied before the arc can be traversed. Actions are executed during the transition through the arc. The network is endowed with a number of registers which store pieces of the final structure produced by the grammar. Tests may examine the content of the registers and actions may assign arbitrary values to them. The forms of the arcs are formalized uniformly and several new arcs are added. The transition network developed in this manner is called the Augmented Transition Network (ATN) and is equivalent in power to a Turing machine.

There exists a variety of formal and quasi-formal descriptions of the ATN model, depending on particular applications, but we would like to present briefly the original and, in our conviction, the most mature version proposed by M. Bates [Bates, 1978]. We will follow her paper, "The Theory and Practice of Augmented Transition Network Grammars", to describe the ATN formalism.

1. Arcs

    (CAT <category> <test> <action>*(TO <next state>))
    (WRD <word> <test> <action>*(TO <next state>))
    (MEM <list> <test> <action>*(TO <next state>))
    (PUSH <state> <test> <pre-action>*<action>*(TO <next state>))
    (VIR <constit-type> <test> <action>*(TO <next state>))
    (JUMP <next state> <test> <action>*
    (POP <form> <test>)

Bates, M. [1978] "The Theory and Practice of Augmented Transition Network Grammars", Lecture Notes in Computer Science, Vol. 63, Bolc, L.(Ed.) "Natural Language Communication with Computers", Springer-Verlag Berlin, Heidelberg, New York

Woods, M.A. [1972] An Experimental Parsing System for Transition Network Grammars, BBN Report No. 2362, Bolt Beranek and Newman Inc. Cambridge, Massachusetts, USA

The meaning of the CAT and WRD arcs was explained above. A MEM arc "is exactly like a WRD arc except that the input word must be one of the list of words which is a second element of the arc" [Bates, 1978]. All the above three arcs "consume" input, that is "they cause the input pointer to be advanced to the next word" [Bates, 1978]. As was mentioned above, a PUSH arc transfers the computation to the indicated state <state> in a recursive manner, interrupting the habitual alternation of the arcs processing.

A sequence of special pre-actions may be placed on that arc which must be executed before the initiation of the lower level computation. Pre-actions can assign initial values to registers on the lower level. When the lower level computation is completed the remaining actions are performed mainly to save the piece of final structure received from the subconstituent just processed.

"A VIR arc checks to see whether a constituent of the named type has been placed on the HOLD list by a HOLD action of some previous arc" [Bates, 1978]. The HOLD/VIR facility is a very important feature of an ATN. The HOLD action may be placed on every arc and causes a piece of information to be added to the special HOLD list under an indicated name. Thus a VIR arc may be traversed when its <constit-type> matches a constituent name on the HOLD list. If the matching is done successfully the constituent is removed from the HOLD list and the traversal is allowed. "The HOLD list is a global list which is accessible at all levels" [Bates, 1978].

At all the above arcs the destination is established by the last action on the arc, that is the TO action; on a JUMP arc it is done by the second element, i.e. <next state>.

A POP arc has no destination. The form is picked up to the higher level of computation as a result of the subnet action. In the top-level net the POP arc gives a final issue of the ATN Grammar. The latter four arcs do not "consume" any input.

2. Actions

    (SETR <reg> <form>)
    (ADDR <reg> <form>)
    (ADDL <reg> <form>)
    (SENDR <reg> <form>)

```
(LIFTR <reg> <form>)
(HOLD <constit-type> <form>)
(VERIFY <form>)
```

The SETR action sets the register <reg> to the value received from the evaluation of <form>. The ADDR and ADDL actions are similar, although ADDL, for example, adds a value of the <form> to the left end of the previous contents of the register <reg> rather than replacing it. The ADDR action is exactly the same except that it adds to the right end. The SENDR action is the pre-action used mainly on PUSH arcs. The LIFTR action is the inverse of SENDR and causes the register <reg> to be set to the value of a form <form> on a level just above the current one. The HOLD action was explained previously. The VERIFY action can break the evaluation of an arc at an arbitrary point. It is a kind of a post-test to examine whether the conditions of the arc being traversed are still holding true or whether they have become false.

3. Forms

   Lex
   *
   (GETR <reg>)
   (GETF <feature> <word>)
   (BUILQ <template> <form>)
   (NULLR <reg>)

A number of different forms may be used in ATN-actions. The most important of them are listed above. "LEX is always set to the current word
of input" [Bates, 1978]. The value of * is the same as LEX on JUMP, POP,
WRD and MEM arcs. "On a CAT arc it is the root form of the word" [Bates,
1978]. This root form is dependent on a dictionary definition and may be
selected arbitrarily by a designer. "On a PUSH arc * is the current input word for the test and pre-actions, but on subsequent actions on the
arc it is the value returned from the lower level computation which was
initiated by the PUSH arc" [Bates, 1978]. It should be added that on a
VIR arc * has the value of a constituent taken off the HOLD list by the
VIR arc. The GETR form returns the contents of the indicated register
<reg>. GETF checks whether the <word> in the dictionary has the feature
<feature> and then returns its value. This action is strongly connected
with the organization of the dictionary. BUILDQ is a form which allows
arbitrary structures to be built. The <template> is a pattern which has
to be filled by values of <forms>. The pattern may consist of a struc-

ture framework and special pattern-slot indicators which are supplied
by register contents and form values. The NULLR action checks whether
or not the indicated register <reg> has a value.

This book is a collection of papers written by well-known scientists
dealing with the problem of Augmented Transition Network Grammars.

The first paper in this volume - "The Planes Interpreter and Compiler
for Augmented Transition Network Grammars" by Timothy Wilking Finin of
the University of Pennsylvania - describes the ATN interpreter and compiler and their implementation in the PLANES natural language query system. PLANES was worked out at the University of Illinois in the 1970's
and supplies the users with a large data base of aircraft maintenance
information.

"An ATN Programming Environment" by Thomas Christaller from Bielefeld
University, West Germany, the second paper in our volume, is devoted
to an ATN system used in the university's Linguistics Department. Attention is concentrated on the individual components of the ATN programming
environment: interpreter, compiler, editor, and debugger.

The third work introduced here is "Compiling Augmented Transition Networks into MACLISP" by Joachim Laubsch of the Open University, Milton
Keynes, England and Karl Barth from the University of Stuttgart. Two
prototypical compilers are described, the first of which, while not being incremental, implements a virtual machine, whereas the second uses
certain control structures of MACLISP to allow for incremental compilation and dynamic loading of the ATN-grammar parts. The authors also deal
with some applications of ATN-grammars.

The last paper in our book, entitled "Towards the Elastic ATN Implementation" by Krzysztof Kochut of Warsaw University, presents two implementations of ATN-grammars. The first, based on Earley's algorithm of parsing context-free languages, enables users to arrive at every parsing
obtainable in one grammar without need for recursive PUSHes to subnets
or backtracking. In his presentation of the second implementation, the
author describes three realizations of what Woods describes as cascaded
ATN-grammars. We are also presented with the motives which led the author
to use this mechanism in natural language analysis. Both these implementations use a simple interpreter and a compiler which cooperates with
it. The last part of the paper describes a simple editor, suitable for

testing and debugging new grammars.

We hope that the works presented in this volume will contribute to further development of Augmented Transition Network grammars.

Warsaw, April 1983   Leonard Bolc

Table of Contents

The Planes Interpreter and Compiler for Augmented Transition Network Grammars [1]

Timothy Wilking Finin [2]

CONTENTS

---

[1] This work was completed while the author was at the Coordinated Science Laboratory of the University of Illinois in Urbana-Champaign.

[2] Department of Computer and Information Science
University of Pennsylvania
Philadelphia, PA 19143 USA

1.0 INTRODUCTION

1.1 The PLANES Natural Language Query System

This chapter discusses the design and implementation of the ATN interpreter and compiler used in the PLANES system ([Walt75], [Walt76] and
[Walt78]). This system, developed at the University of Illinois in the
mid 70's, is an interactive question answering system which answers
questions concerning a large data base of aircraft maintenance information. The intended scope of the PLANES system is to answer such questions as:

> How many Skyhawks required engine repairs in 1973?
> Did any of these log more than 200 hours in March?
> Show me the tail numbers of planes which were NOR during May.
> What kinds of aircraft are in the data base?

The processing of a user's request is divided into three main phases:
parsing, interpretation, and evaluation (see figure 1 - The PLANES System).

The first phase, the parsing, is driven by a large ATN grammar. This
ATN grammar defines a "semantic grammar" [Brow76] which maps the users
request into an internal representation, the Paraphrase Language. The
grammar is "semantic" in that it incorporates semantic and pragmatic
knowledge as well as syntactic.

The Paraphrase Language representation of the user's request is translated by the second stage into a 'program' to generate the data to answer the request. This stage contains detailed knowledge about the data
bases. It must know, for example, which sub-parts of the data base contain certain relations and the particular codes used to represent certain facts. The program is constructed out of primitives provided by
the Query Language.

Finally, the Query Language evaluates the 'program' and passes the resulting data to the Response Generator. This module can display the answer in one of three forms: as a simple number or list, as a graph, or as
a table. The choice of output form can be determined by the user thru a
direct request (e.g. "Draw a graph of ...") or by a set of heuristics
which attempt to find the most "natural" form. A graph, for example,
will be generated only if the data consists of a set of tuples which

4

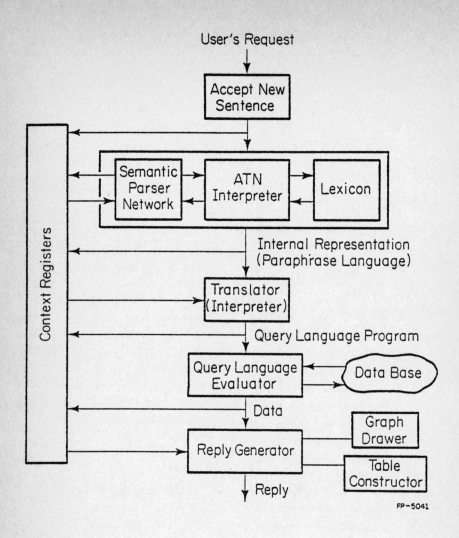

User's Request

Accept New Sentence

Context Registers

Semantic Parser Network

ATN Interpreter

Lexicon

Internal Representation (Paraphrase Language)

Translator (Interpreter)

Query Language Program

Query Language Evaluator

Data Base

Data

Reply Generator

Graph Drawer

Table Constructor

Reply

FP-5041

Fig.: 1 The PLANES System

can be interpreted as a function of two variables. Furthermore, the number of tuples must lie within certain bounds.

At each stage of the process, the results are sent to the History Keeper which manages a set of stacks of relevant information. These stacks contain the results of each stage (e.g. users request, paraphrase, etc.), syntactic components (e.g. subject, object, etc.), and semantic/contextual information (e.g. time specifications, plane specifications, etc.). This information is made available for resolving anaphoric reference, supplying phrases deleted thru ellipsis, and generating responses.

The entire process can be aborted by any of the major stages. If this is done, a suitable error message is generated and the user is invited to reform his request.

1.2 An Overview of this Chapter

This chapter describes the design and use of the PLANES ATN system. An earlier version ([Fini77a]) in fact, also served as a user's manual. Section 2 gives a brief description of ATN's and discusses some of the high level design considerations. Section 3 describes the interpreter and the auxiliary functions available to the user in some detail. Section 4 presents the compiler which can translate ATN networks into LISP code or machine language instructions. Section 5 describes the dictionary format expected by the interpreter. Also discussed are the various functions provided for creating and maintaining dictionaries. Section 6 documents several packages of auxiliary functions provided for interfacing the ATN system with the LISP editor and Pretty-printer. The chapter closes with examples of a very simple English grammar, a dictionary, and traces of the application of this grammar and dictionary to parsing some simple sentences.

1.3 Conventions

This chapter documents many LISP functions and "function-like" constructions. As part of the description for a function, a "syntax frame" will be given which specifies the number of arguments and whether or not they are evaluated. A "syntax frame" will look like a typical call to the function, i.e. it will be a list whose first element is the name of the function and whose remaining elements are the arguments. Arguments in the "syntax frame" will typically be enclosed in angle-brackets (<,>).

For example, the syntax frame for the LISP function LESSP might be:

        (LESSP <number> <number>)

which states that LESSP takes two arguments, both of which are evaluated.

If a quote-sign (') precedes an argument, then that argument is not evaluated by the function. For example, the following describes the function DEFPROP:

        (DEFPROP '<atom> '<value> '<property>)

If a function takes one or more optional arguments, then several "syntax frames" will be given. For example, the MacLISP function CATCH would
be described as:

        (CATCH <expression> '<tag>)
        (CATCH <expression>)

Two conventions will be used to exhibit functions which take an indefinite number of arguments. In one, the arguments are simply partially
enumerated with the elliptical "...", as in:

        (PLUS <number1> <number2> ... <number n>)

The second form has the last argument to the function preceded by the
"dotted pair" dot, as in:

        (DEFUN '<name> '<argument list> . '<function body>)

The last argument then stands for an indefinite number of final arguments. Example calls to a function will usually be given with the "syntax frame" to clarify its usage. These will be preceded by an "eg:" indicator.

2.0 AUGMENTED TRANSITION NETWORKS

2.1 Introduction

The ATN formalism has been well received by the computational linguistics community in the past decade. A number of people were working with
similar models in the late 60's (see [Thor68] and [Bobr69]), but the
idea was crystallized and popularized by the work of William Woods in
the early 70's [Wood71]. The ATN model has been heavily used to represent grammars for question answering systems, speech processing systems,

language generation systems, modeling learning and even for processing
visual information [Loza77]. This section will provide a brief introduction to the ATN formalism. An excellent introduction to the theory
and use of ATN grammars can be found in [Bate79].

2.2 The ATN Formalism

The ATN formalism is usually described in a evolutionary manner, showing
how one can start with the notion of a simple finite state machine (FSM)
and modify and embellish it to arrive at an Augmented Finite State Transition Network (ASFTN).

The FSM is the basis for ATN's

We start with a garden variety deterministic FSM consisting of a set of
labeled states, a set of arcs between states, an initial state, and a
set of distinguished final or accepting states. The first step might be
to extend the formalism to allow for non-determinism. A simple grammar
for English might be represented by the graph in figure 2 (A Simple
Grammar for English). As a model for natural language processing this
is inadequate. The most serious deficit is the lack of any mechanism to
handle embedding of constituents to arbitrary depth. The next extension,
then, is to provide a "push down" mechanism whereby one can suspend the
processing of a constituent at one level while using the same network
to process an embedded one.

Adding recursion extends the power of an FSM

We can represent this by labeling an arc from one state to another with
the name of a third state. When such an arc is encountered, processing
is suspended and the network restarted in the specified state. If an
accepting state is eventually reached, the suspended processing is resumed. Such a capability not only allows one to achieve the power to
parse a context free language, but also simplifies the representation
of a grammar. One can collect common network fragments and specify them
in one place, much as one can substitute a subroutine call for common
program sequences in a programming language. Our simplistic English
grammar might now be represented by the graph in figure 3 (A Better
Grammar for English). Note that this grammar now accepts conjoined sentences and sentences embedded as relative clauses.

Augmentation realizes the power of ATN's

8

Fig. 2: A Simple Grammar for English

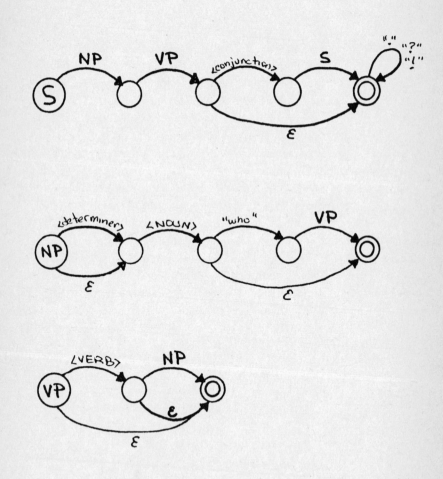

Fig. 3: A Better Grammar for English

Whether or not recursive transition networks provide a theoretically
adaquate mechanism for parsing natural languages is an open question.
It is clear, however, that from a practical viewpoint, the RTN formalism is not as powerful as one would like it to be. To further extend
the power of our formalism we will allow arcs to be augmented with conditions and actions. Each arc can be augmented with:

1. An arbitrary condition which must be met before the arc
   may be taken.

2. A set of arbitrary actions which will be performed if the
   arc is taken. These can have side effects thru the setting
   of registers whose contents can later be accessed in other
   parts of the grammar.

This augmentation (among others) gives an ATN the computational power
of a Turing machine. The final result is a powerful formalism which re-
tains much of the elegance of the simple FSM.

2.3 Design Considerations

Since ATN's are based on non-deterministic FSM's, an implementation must
be able to simulate all possible paths thru the network. We have chosen
to implement a depth-first backtracking version for several reasons.
Firstly, it is our belief that natural language processing may be most
suited to this approach. At least, evidence suggests that our only example of competent natural language processors (i.e. humans) do not use
highly parallel methods. Secondly, we believe that whatever gains might
be made thru a parallel approach would be more than offset by the additional cost of processing. The phenomenon of natural language is such
that it encompasses an extraordinarily large number of patterns and constructions. Most of these, however, are relatively rare, the greatest
part of most language being drawn from a few common constructions. A
non-parallel approach can easily take advantage of this fact in the or-
dering of its attempts to find a path thru the ATN network.

To simulate the non-deterministic nature of an ATN processor (or a FSM
for that matter) one needs to maintain an encoding of the current configuration (i.e. state, input word, register environment, etc.) as well
as a stack of past configurations which represent the path so far. In
our ATN system, we have chosen a recursive implementation in which this
information is stored on LISP's internal stack. The alternative is to

maintain an explicit configuration stack built from CONS cells from the
general pool. The advantages of a recursive implementation include:

o Simplicity of design

   Backing up to a previous configuration is achieved by
   "returning" to the environment of that configuration.
   The undoing of side-effects is automatic.

o Efficiency

   Previous configurations are stored on LISP's internal
   stack and thus do not consume CONS cells from the general
   pool. This reduces the amount of LIST space required and,
   more importantly, results in fewer and shorter garbage
   collections.

The chief disadvantage of a recursive implementation is that we give up
the possibility of giving the user complete control over processing.
Earlier configurations are inaccessible to the user as well as to the
system itself (*). This problem is alleviated by the inclusion of several flow-of-control modifiers thru which one can directly fail back to
a specified configuration.

2.4 Implementation

The PLANES ATN interpreter, Dictionary Manager, and ATN compiler are
written in the LISP dialect MacLisp, which runs on a variety of machines
and operating systems (**). PDP-10 TOPS10 timesharing system. The following gives approximate values for memory requirements:

	LIST space	BPS space
Interpreter	5100	4000
Dictionary Manager	1200	1000
Compiler	2500	1500

In this table, LIST space refers to the number of memory cells used to

---

(*) This makes certain kinds of parallel processing regimes difficult,
     if not impossible, to implement.

(**) Versions of MacLisp exist for PDP-10s under the TOPS-a0, TOPS-20,
     ITS, and WAIT operating systems and for MULTICS. Two other Lisp
     dialects are sufficiently close to MacLisp to allow the PLANES ATN
     system to run with minor modifications: FranzLisp (for a PDP11/780
     Vax) and Lisp Machine Lisp.

store lists, atoms, etc. and BPS space refers to 'Binary Program Space', the number of memory cells used to store compiled code.

<u>3.0 THE ATN INTERPRETER</u>

This section describes the principal functions in the PLANES ATN interpreter.

3.1 Invoking the ATN Interpreter

<u>PARSE</u> and <u>PARSE1</u> <u>invoke</u> <u>the</u> <u>interpreter</u>

PARSE and PARSE1 are the main functions used to invoke the ATN interpreter on an input string. The function PARSE is intended to be used at LISP's toplevel and PARSE1 used by other programs.

(PARSE '<string> '<initial state> '<number of parses>)

    eg: (PARSE (which skyhawks required repairs) s:start 3)

The function PARSE starts the ATN interpreter in state <initial state> with the input string <string>. It takes from 0 to 3 arguments, none of which is evaluated. If any argument is omitted or is NIL, it is defaulted as specified below.

The first argument specifies the input string to be parsed. If it is a list of atoms, then that list is used as the input string. If it is an atom which has a value, then the value of the atom is used as the input string. If it is omitted or is NIL, then the function READTEXT is called which reads the input string from the terminal. The second argument to PARSE specifies the initial state of an ATN network. If it is omitted or NIL, it defaults to the value of the global variable @INITIALSTATE. The third argument determines how many parses are produced. If it is omitted or NIL, it defaults to one. If it is a positive number, then the interpreter will attempt to produce that many parses. If it is the atom ALL, then all possible parses will be produced.

The function PARSE always returns the value "*", so it is run for its side-effects. The principle side-effect is that it sets the variable PARSE to:

    o The atom FAIL if the ATN was unable to reach a final state.

o The value POPped by the ATN if <number of parses> is 1.

o A list of the values POPped if <number of parses> is greater than one or the atom ALL.

In addition, this value is "pretty printed" on the terminal and the atom AGAIN is set to the input string.

(PARSE1 <string> <initial state> <number of parses>)

   eg: (PARSE1 '(show me the list) 's:start 'all)

The function PARSE1 requires all three arguments, each of which is evaluated. It returns the value(s) POPped by the ATN from the final state(s). PARSE1 has the side-effect of binding the global variable AGAIN to <in­put string>.

(READTEXT)

If the first argument to PARSE is omitted or NIL, the function READTEXT is called to read the input string from the TTY. This function reads a string of characters from the TTY until a carriage-return is typed and returns it in the form of a list of atoms. Characters which have a "special" meaning to LISP (e.g. . , ; , etc.) are automatically "slashified" (i.e. taken literally).

The function incorporates three special features:

1. If the null string is entered by typing only a carriage-return, then READTEXT returns the last input string given to PARSE (i.e. the value of AGAIN).

2. If the first character on the line is a "(" then READTEXT reads a LISP s-expression, evaluates it, and prints the resulting value. It then waits for a string of characters to be typed as the input string.

3. Whenever a line-feed is typed, READTEXT takes the next character of the input string from the last input string (AGAIN again). Subsequent line-feeds produce subsequent characters from the old input string.

3.2 Arc Types

The PLANES ATN interpreter provides a total of 13 varieties of arcs.

These can be broken down into the following categories:

1. Flow of Control (PUSH, POP, TO, JUMP, FAIL)

   These are arcs which effect transitions from one state to another or invoke or return from sub-computations.

2. Testing the Current Word (CAT, WRD, ROOT, PHRASE)

   These arcs are taken only when the current word meets a specified condition.

3. Virtual Arc (VIR)

   This arc provides a natural mechanism for handling constituents which are parsed "out of place" in the input string.

4. Miscellaneous Arcs (TST, DO, AND)

   These three arcs provide a mechanism for miscellaneous computation.

All of the arcs except the AND arc have the basic form:

    (<type> <head> <test> <action1> ... <actionn>)

where <type> is one of the arc types (PUSH, CAT, TST, etc.), <head> is an argument for that arc type, <test> is an arbitrary condition which must be met before the arc can be taken, and the <actions>'s are arbitrary lisp expressions which are evaluated if the arc is taken. Typically the last action will specify destination - the next state to go to.

3.2.1 Arcs which Test the Current Word

The WRD arc compares the current word

```
(WRD '<word(s)> <test> ... <actions> ... <destination>)
eg: (WRD (the a) T (SETR det *)(TO np:det))
    (WRD please t (SETR polite t)(TO s:start))
```

The WRD arc compares the current word against <word(s)>, which can be an atom or a list of atoms. If the current word matches, then <test> is evaluated and, if true, the actions are evaluated from left to right.

The CAT arc checks for a lexical category

```
(CAT '<head> <test> ... <actions> ... <destination>)
eg: (CAT adj T (ADDR adj *)(TO np:adj))
    (CAT (n npr) t (SETR n *)(TO np:n))
```

A CAT arc is taken if the current word has a lexical entry under the category <head> (if it is an atom) or any of the categories <head> if a
list. Within the CAT arc, the variable * is bound to the root form of
the current word. For example, if the current word is CRASHING, then the
following arc would set the register VERB to CRASH:

```
(CAT V T (SETR verb *)(TO s:verb))
```

Note that this arc may generate several possibilities if the current
word has more than one dictionary entry under the specified category.
For example, the word SAW might have the dictionary entry:

```
(SAW V  (SEE (tns past))
        (SAW (tns present)(untensed)))
```

In this case the CAT arc above will first try parsing SAW as the past
tense of SEE and, if that fails, will try parsing SAW as the present/
untensed form of the verb SAW.

The ROOT arc checks the root form

```
(ROOT '<root(s)> <test> ... <actions> ... <destination>)
eg: (ROOT BE T (SETR v *)(to S:BE))
    (ROOT (have be) (NULLR aux)(SETR aux *)(TO s:aux))
```

A ROOT arc compares the root form of the current word to <root(s)>.
Again, <root(s)> can be an atom or a list of atoms. The arc is taken
if the current word matches one of the forms in <root(s)> . As with the
CAT arc, the variable * is bound to the root form of the current word
within the ROOT arc.

The PHRASE arc checks the next several words

```
(PHRASE '<phrase> <test> ... <actions> ... <destination>)
eg: (PHRASE (more or less) T (SETR fuzzy T)(TO quant:end))
    (PHRASE (please (give show tell) (me {})) T (TO s:imperative))
```

The PHRASE arc is used to compare the next several words in the input
string to <phrase>, which should be a list. Successive elements of
<phrase> are matched against successive words from the input string.

The possibilities for phrase elements, and what they represent are given below:

o A simple word (e.g. MORE)

   The given word must match the corresponding word in the input stream exactly.

o A root form (e.g. {eat})

   A word between "{" and "}" specifies a root form match. The root form of the corresponding word in the input must match the given root. If the input word has several different root forms (corresponding to several lexical categories) then the given root may match any one of them.

o A lexical category (e.g. {.prep})

   A word between "{." and "}" indicates a lexical category to compare the next input word to. If the input word is a member of the specified category, then the phrase match continues.

o A list of Phrase elements (e.g. ({give} {show} {tell}))

   An element which is a list enumerates several possibilities for the corresponding word in the input string. If any one of them matches the next input word, then the match continues.

The phrase arc is taken if and only if each element of <phrase> is successfully matched against the input string.

3.2.2 Arcs which Modify the Flow of Control

These arc types can be further divided into arcs which involve sub-computations (PUSH, POP, POP!), arcs effecting state transitions (TO, JUMP) and an arc which controls backtracking (FAIL).

The PUSH arc invokes a sub-computation

```
(Push '<state> <test> ... <actions> ... <destination>)
eg:  (PUSH np t (SENDR goal 'subj)(SETR subj *)(TO s:subj))
```

The PUSH arc is used to invoke a sub-computation. If the expression <test> is true, then the ATN interpreter is recursively called, starting in state <state>. All registers at the current level are saved and made invisible to the lower level. Before actually invoking the lower level, the list of actions is scanned for "preactions", i.e. those which should be evaluated before the PUSH is made. These "preactions" are SENDR's or any action which begins with a "!" (e.g. (! (OR (EQ Sv 'be) (SENDR v))). The SENDR actions, and any previously done, are typically used to set register values in the lower computation.

If the sub-computation fails, i.e. does not reach a state which can take a POP arc, then the PUSH fails. If a POP from the lower level is taken, then control is returned to the PUSH arc. The variable * is then set to the value POPped by the lower network, the values of any LIFTRed registers set, and the "post-actions" evaluated. These "post-actions" are just the actions on the arc minus the "pre-actions".

The POP arc returns from a sub-computation

(POP <value> <test> . <actions>)

The POP arc returns from a sub-computation. If <test> is true, the <actions> are evaluated from left to right and then <value> is computed and returned to the most recent PUSH arc or PUSHATN action. Both <test> and <actions> can be omitted. If the <test> argument is omitted, it defaults to T.

Two conditions affect the taking of a POP arc. If any items were on the HOLD list at this level and have not yet been used, then the POP arc can not be taken (see section 2.5.5). In addition, a POP arc will not be taken if it would be returning to the "top-level" and words remain to be parsed (i.e. STRING is non-NIL). This last condition can be turned off if the global variable USE-ALL-WORDS? is set to NIL.

Some examples of POP arcs are:

(POP (build-np) T (LIFTR head-noun $noun))
(POP (BUILDQ (pp + +) prep np))

The POP! arc really returns

(POP! <value> <test> . <actions>)

The POP! arc is almost identical to the POP arc except for one important difference: one can not back-up into the sub-computation after leaving it via a POP! arc. Under our implementation of the ATN interpreter, a POP! arc does a RETURN to the environment of the most recent PUSH arc or call to the PUSHATN action. If failure later backs up to this point, the entire sub-computation will, in effect, be backed up over as well.

The grammar writer may find this a useful arc in that it gives him greater control over the automatic backtracking done by the ATN interpreter.

The TO and JUMP arcs effect state transitions

```
(TO '<state> <test> . <actions>)
(JUMP '<state> <test> . <actions>)
```

As a convenience, special arcs are provided which duplicate the TO and JUMP actions. Both arc types cause the ATN interpreter to advance to the state specified by their first "argument". The TO arc causes the current word to be advanced and the JUMP arc does not. In each case, the <test> argument and the <actions> arguments are optional. If the <test> is omitted, it defaults to T. Some examples are:

```
(JUMP s:end (out-of-words?))
(JUMP np:det)
(TO np:det t (ADDR ignored-words *))
```

The FAIL arc controls backtracking

```
(FAIL '<where> <test> . <actions>)
```

The FAIL arc can be used to gain some control over backtracking. If the <test> is true, then this arc will evaluate the <actions> and cause failure to propagate backwards to a point specified by <where>. Again, the <test> and <actions> arguments may be omitted.

The <where> argument may specify that the ATN interpreter fail from the current arc, the current state, the current sub-computation, an arbitrary named state, or to the initial top-level call. The precise options for the <where> argument are:

```
STATE   : fail from the current state
PUSH    : fail from the current subcomputation
          (i.e. from the most recent PUSH)
<state> : fail from the named state
TOP     : fail altogether
```

Note that the setting of registers in the <actions> will have no effect since their side effects will be immediately undone by the failure. Some examples of FAIL arcs are:

```
(FAIL state)
(FAIL np:adj (CAT v))
(FAIL push (NOT (CAT prep)))
```

3.2.3 The Virtual Arc

```
(VIR '<cat> <test> ... <actions> ... <destination>)
(VIR '(<cat> <level>) <test> ... <actions> ... <destination>)
```

The VIR or virtual arc is taken if a constituent is found on the HOLD list indexed under the category <cat>. Again, the <test> argument must evaluate to non-NIL.

Note that two syntax frames are given for this arc. In the first, the "head" of a VIR arc is an atomic category name. In the second, it is a tuple whoes first element is a category name and whose second is a number which specifies the level at which the constituent is to be found on the HOLD list. See section 3.5.5 for details.

If the VIR arc can be taken, * is bound to the constituent found on the HOLD list and FEATURES is bound to the (optional) feature list associated with that constituent.

3.2.4 Miscellaneous Arcs

The TST arc applies an arbitrary test

```
(TST '<label> <test> ... <actions> ... <destination>)
```

The TST arc is taken if the arbitrary LISP expression <test> evaluates to non-NIL. The <label> argument is not evaluated and is not used in any way by the ATN interpreter. Typically it is used for a mnemonic label describing the function of the arc. Some examples are:

```
(TST end-of-sent? (AND (NULL *)(NULL string))(JUMP s:end))
(TST t (MEMQ   cuss-words)(TO s:complain))
```

The DO arc has no destination

```
(DO '<label> <test> . <actions>)
```

The ATN interpreter handles the DO arc in an identical manner to the TST arc. If the <test> is true, the <actions> are evaluated. Its intended use, however, is somewhat different. The TST arc is intended to have a "destination action" as its final action (i.e. a call to TO or JUMP). The DO arc is intended to be used without a "destination action". Thus, the DO arc might be used to initialize a set of registers. Some sample DO arcs are given below:

```
(DO initialize t (SETR type 'dcl)(SETR context NIL)
(DO warn verbose? (print '|That is not very grammatical!|))
```

The AND arc conjoins other arcs

```
(AND <arc1> <arc2> ... <arcn>)
```

The AND arc is the only one which does not fit the general arc syntax.
The AND arc takes an indefinite number of arguments, each of which can
be any of the legal arc types (including another AND arc). The effect
of an AND arc is to evaluate each of the "sub-arcs" from left to right
until one of them fails or the last one is reached. Consequently, none
of the "sub-arcs" should contain a "destination action" except the last
one, which should have a "destination" as its last action.

Note that after evaluating each of the "sub-arcs", the current word is
always advanced. This arc is useful in eliminating many states which
contain only a single arc. This can greatly increase the readability of
a network by keeping together arcs which form a single path. For example,
to handle two-word comparative adjective, one might use the following
arc:

```
(AND (WRD more t)
        (CAT adj t (SETR adj (BUILDQ (adj: * comparative)))
                (TO np:adj)))
```

3.3 Defining ATN Networks and States

The PLANES ATN system provides functions for defining ATN networks,
states, individual arcs and special word-triggered interrupt functions.

DEFATN defines an ATN network

```
(DEFATN '<name> '<default-arcs> '<default-registers>
        '(<state> ... <state>))
```

The function DEFATN takes from 2 to 4 arguments and defines an ATN network. The first argument is the name of the ATN network and the last
argument is a list of the states in the network. Intervening arguments
are optional and, if included, can specify initial values for registers
and special "default arcs" which are assumed to be the initial arcs of
each state in the network.

If a register default argument is supplied, its form should be:

```
("default-register" (<register name> <value>)
                    (<register name> <value>)
                    ... ))
```

This argument causes the named registers to be set to the specified initial values whenever a state in the network is PUSHed to.

If a "default-arc" argument is given to DEFATN, its form should be:

```
("default-arc"  <arc1> <arc2> ... <arcn>)
```

where an arc has one of the forms:

```
<arc name>
(<arc type> <head>.... )
```

If the arc is an atom, it is assumed to be the name of separately defined arc (see DEFARC). If it is a list, then it should be in the form of a legally defined arc. The effect of this argument is to cause the specified arcs to be added at the beginning of each state in the network.

DEFSTATE defines an individual state

```
(DEFSTATE '<name> . '<arcs>)
```

Individual ATN states can be defined with the function DEFSTATE. This function takes an indefinite number of arguments, the first of which is the name of the state. The remaining arguments specify the arcs leading from the state. Again, an arc can be represented either by an atomic name or by a complete list. An example is:

```
(DEFSTATE np:start
    (CAT det (SETR det *)(TO np:det))
    (CAT pro (SETR noun *)(TO np:end))
    (JUMP np:det))
```

DEFARC defines an individual arc

```
(DEFARC '<name> '<arc>)
```

An individual arc can be defined with the function DEFARC. Arcs defined in this way can be of two types: Regular arcs which have a destination

(i.e. a call to TO or JUMP) as their last action and degenerate arcs
which do not have a destination as their last action. When a degenerate
arc is inserted into an ATN state, a destination is supplied which causes
the ATN to loop back to that state. For example:

```
(DEFARC timephrase (PUSH timepp T (SETR time *)))
```

is an arc which will attempt to parse a time phrase and then reenter the
current state.

Word interrupts are created by DEFINTERUPT

The PLANES ATN system provides a mechanism whereby certain computations
can be performed whenever a certain word is encountered in the input
string. The function DEFINTERUPT associates an interrupt function with
a word.

```
(DEFINTERUPT '<word(s)> '<function>)
 eg: (DEFINTERUPT please cdr)
     (DEFINTERUPT (in on before)
                   (lambda (x)(parse-time-pp (car x)(cdr x))))
```

The first argument to DEFINTERUPT should be a word or a list of words.
The second should be a function of one argument, expressed as either
the atomic name of the function or as a lambda expression. Whenever one
of the specified words is encountered in the input string, the associated interrupt function is called with the input string as its argument.
Its return value is used as the new input string. Thus the first example
would cause the word PLEASE to be ignored (since it returns the CDR of
the input string). The second example would call the function PARSE-
TIME-PP whenever the words IN, ON, or BEFORE are discovered in the input string.

3.4 Functions for Manipulating Registers

A register in an ATN grammar plays the role of a variable in a higher
level programming system. The interpreter provides functions for assigning a register a value (SETR, SENDR, LIFTR), accessing the value of a
register (GETR,$), and testing the contents of a register (NULLR). Re-
gisters need not be declared and are "created" when they are assigned
a value for the first time. The contents of a register which has never
been assigned a value is defined to be NIL.

3.4.1 Setting Registers

Registers can be set at the current level (SETR) in the next lower level (SENDR) or in any of the higher levels (LIFTR).

SETR sets a register at the current level

(SETR '<register name> <value>)
 eg: (SETR verb 'be)

The function SETR assigns a value to a register at the current level. SETR assigns the register <register name> the value <value>.

SENDR sets a register at a lower level

(SENDR '<register name> <value>)
(SENDR '<register name>)

SENDR is used to set the contents of a register at a lower level, typically just before a PUSH action. Whenever a SENDR is evaluated, the register name and value are stored on the SENDLIST. When a PUSH occurs, the SENDLIST is used to initialize the registers to the specified values. If the second argument is omitted, it defaults to the current contents of the register named by the first argument. Thus (SENDR noun) is the equivalent to (SENDR noun (GETR noun)).

LIFTR sets a register at a higher level

The function LIFTR is used to set the contents of a register at a higher level. It takes from one to three arguments, the syntax being:

    (LIFTR '<register name> <value> <level>)
    (LIFTR '<register name> <value>)
    (LIFTR '<register name>)

If all three arguments are given, LIFTR assigns <register name> the value <value> <level> levels above the current one. For example, (LIFTR stype 'q 1) would set the register STYPE to Q in the next higher level. If the <level> argument is the atom TOP, then it refers to the highest level. If the <level> argument is omitted, it defaults to 1 (i.e. the next higher level).

The second argument, <value>, specifies the value to be assigned to the register. If it is omitted, the current contents of the register are used. Thus (LIFTR noun) is equivalent to (LIFTR noun (GETR noun)).

When a LIFTR action is evaluated, it adds the complete three tuple (<register name><value><level>) to the special register LIFTLIST. When a POP action is taken, the LIFTLIST is processed by setting those registers associated with a <level> of 1 and "re-lifting" the rest of the elements with a decremented <level>. Thus, the effect of a LIFTR is only seen once we have POPped to the appropriate level.

3.4.2 Accessing Registers

GETR gets the contents of a register

The function GETR is used to access the contents of a register at the current level or, if an optional argument is supplied, at any higher level. The syntax is:

```
(GETR '<register name>)
(GETR '<register name> <level>)
(GETR '<register name> 'nearest <test>)
```

If only one argument is supplied, GETR retrieves the contents of that register at the current level. An optional second argument instructs GETR to get the contents of the register at a higher level. In addition, if <level> evaluates to the atom NEAREST, then GETR will return the contents of the register at the lowest level in which it has a value. If <level> is NEAREST, an optional third argument, <test>, can specify an arbitrary test which must be met by the candidate register value. While evaluating <test>, the variable * is bound to the contents of the candidate register. For example, the expression:

```
(GETR verb 'nearest '(TRANSITIVE *))
```

would search upwards thru the chain of levels until it found a VERB register which contained a transitive verb (assuming that TRANSITIVE is a user-defined predicate which is true of transitive verbs only).

The character $ acts as prefix operator

The character $ (i.e. dollar sign) is defined to be a "read macro character" which acts as a prefix operator identical to GETR. Thus $noun is the equivalent to the function call (GETR noun). This feature can be turned on or off with the function DOLLARMACRO. Evaluating (DOLLARMACRO NIL) will turn it off causing the dollar sign to lose its special significance. Similarly, (DOLLARMACRO T) will turn the feature back on.

3.4.3 Testing the Contents of a Register

NULLR tests the value of a register

Since the value of a register which has never been set is defined to be NIL, there is no way to tell whether or not a register has been set to the value NIL or has never been set. To provide the user with this capability, the function NULLR will return T if and only if a register has been explicitly set to NIL. The syntax is simply:

    (NULLR '<register name>)

3.5 Flow of Control

Six function are provided which modify the flow of control. Five of them are analogous to arcs PUSH, POP, TO, JUMP and FAIL. The sixth provides a special facility by which one can save the state of a subcomputation just before returning via a POP and later resume it with the same register environment.

3.5.1 Effecting State Transitions

TO and JUMP advance the ATN to a new state

These are typically found as the last action at the end of an arc, as in:

    (CAT v t (SETR v *)(TO s:verb))
    (TST T (out-of-words)(JUMP s:end))

They can, however, be called at any point by the user and embedded in arbitrary LISP expressions. For example, the destination of the following arc is determined at run-time:

    (CAT v t (setr v *) (cond ((transitive ⌀v) (TO s:verb-trans))
                             ((TO s:verb-interans)))))

(TO '<state name>)
 eg: (TO s:verb)

The TO function effects a transition to the named state and causes the current word to be advanced.

```
(JUMP '<state name>)
 eg: (JUMP s:end)
```

The JUMP function also causes the ATN interpreter to enter the specified state but does <u>not</u> advance the input word. The next state will find
the current word unchanged.

3.5.2 Invoking and Returning from Sub-computations

<u>PUSHATN</u> <u>simulates</u> <u>a</u> <u>PUSH</u>

```
(PUSHATN <state>)
 eg: (PUSHATN np:start)
```

The effect of a call to the function PUSHATN is similar to that of a
PUSH arc. It recursively applies the ATN network to the input string
starting in state <state>. The value returned by this function is the
value POPed by the sub-computation or the atom FAIL if the sub-computation does not reach a final state. Additional side-effects are:

  o   The variable * is bound to the value POPped.

  o   The variable LEX is bound to the new current word.

  o   The variable STRING is bound to the rest of the input string.

<u>POPATN</u> <u>simulates</u> <u>a</u> <u>POP</u>

```
(POPATN <value>)
 eg: (POPATN (buildquestion))
```

The POPATN function is similar to the POP arc. It causes control to re-
turn to the most recent PUSH arc or PUSHATN function call. As with the
POP arc, the POP will only succeed if nothing has been placed on the
HOLD list at the current level.

3.5.3 Controlling Backtracking and Failure

<u>FAIL</u> <u>controls</u> <u>backtracking</u>

```
(FAIL <where>)
```

The FAIL function is almost identical to the FAIL arc. It causes the
ATN interpreter to backtrack to a point specified by the argument
<where>. The options for this argument are:

```
ARC      : fail from the current arc
*        : fail from the current state
PUSH     : fail from current level (i.e. to most recent PUSH)
TOP      : fail from entire network (i.e. give up completely)
<state>  : fail back to the state named <state>
```

3.5.4 Suspending and Resuming Computations

Suppose that we wanted to parse a sentence like:

How many planes were there which required no repairs in April?

In this sentence, the relative clause "which required no repairs in April" has been extraposed to the right (or the head "how many planes" extraposed to the left, if you like). We would like to be able to parse these two sub-strings as if they occurred together, as is usually the case:

... planes which required no maintenance in April ...

Using RESUME and RESUMETAG, one can "remember" where one stopped parsing a noun phrase (e.g. in "How many planes") and, at some later point in the input string, resume parsing the same noun phrase in the same state and with the same register environment.

RESUMETAG saves a configuration

```
(RESUMETAG '<state name>)
(RESUMETAG)
```

The RESUMETAG function returns a "tag" which encodes a state name and a register environment. With this "tag", one can later resume computation in this state with the same register environment. If the <state name> argument is not given, the current state is used.

RESUME resumes a suspended computation

```
(RESUME <tag> . '<register names>)
 eg: (RESUME ∅nptag verb)
```

The RESUME function resumes the subcomputation which generated <tag> (i.e. with a call to RESUMETAG) in the current position in the input string. Optional arguments to RESUME specify registers whose contents should be "sent" to the lower computation. The value returned by RESUME is the value POPped by the lower level.

3.5.5 The HOLD/VIRTUAL Facility

The HOLD action together with the VIR arc provide a natural mechanism
for handling constituents which are parsed "out of place" in a sentence.
The HOLD action allows one to place a parsed constituent on the HOLD
list. At some later time, the VIR arc can be used to retrieve the held
object and process it as if it were found at that point in the input
string.

An example will show the usefulness of this facility. English syntax
allows for the fronting of the "unknown element" in a question (e.g. a
wh-noun phrase such as "who" or "which man". One would probably like a
grammar to locate the place from which the unknown element was fronted.
One strategy, then, is to place the unknown constituent on the HOLD list
(via the HOLD action) and then write the grammar such that it checks the
HOLD list whenever it can't find a constituent in the input string.

For example, consider the following sentences:

    Who did John see?
    Who did John sit next to?
    Who did John believe that Harry saw?
    Who does John think the FBI wanted to arrest?

These sentences can be handled by placing the constituent generated by
the "who" on the HOLD list indexed as a Noun Phrase. At each point in
the grammar where a NP is sought as either the subject of a sentence,
the object of a sentence, or the object of a preposition, we include a
VIR arc which examines the HOLD list for a held NP.

The addition of the HOLD/VIRTUAL concept to a RTN extends its power by
providing, in essence, an additional stack. The ATN grammar in figure 4,
for example, accepts the context-sensitive language

$$S \rightarrow a^n b^n c^n$$

The HOLD action

(HOLD <form> <cat> <features>)
 eg: (HOLD * 'np nil)

The HOLD action places the expression <form> on the HOLD list indexed
under the category <cat>. An optional third argument, <features> is a

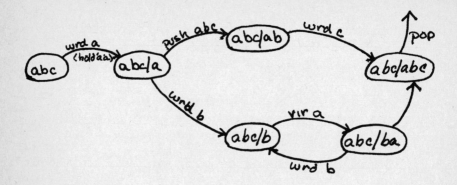

```
(defatn anbncn

       (abc (wrd a t (hold 'a 'a) (to abc/a)))

       (abc/a (wrd b t (to abc/b))
              (push abc t (to abc/ab)))

       (abc/ab (wrd c t (to abc/abc)))

       (abc/abc (pop t))

       (abc/b (vir a t (to abc/ba)))

       (abc/ba (wrd c t (to abc/abc))
               (wrd b t (to abc/b))))
```

Fig. 4: A Grammar for $a^n b^n c^n$

list of features to be associated with the entry. In addition, the level at which this action is being done is recorded with the entry. This allows a VIR arc to select only those constituents held at a particular level.

The VIRtual arc

The VIR arc allows the grammar to retrieve an element from the HOLD list. In retrieving the element, the user can specify:

o The lexical category under which the element was held.

o A limit on the number of levels above the current one at which the element was held.

o An arbitrary test which the element or its features must pass.

The syntax frame for the VIR arc is:

(VIR <head> <test> ... <actions> ... <destination>)

where <head> can have either of the following two forms:

<cat>
(<cat> <level>)

The first form will match any item on the HOLD list indexed under the category <cat> regardless of the level at which it was held. In the second form, <level> specifies the level(s) at which a candidate item was held. This argument should be a number (O or positive) which limits the number of levels above the current one at which the item was held. Thus:

(VIR (PP O) ...)

will match items indexed as a PP which were held at the current level only. Similarly,

(VIR (ADV 2) ...)

would find ADV's held at the current level or the next two higher levels.

Once a candidate match has been found, the <test> argument is evaluated in an environment where * is bound to the candidate constituent and FEATURES is bound to the (optional) features list associated with it. If <test> is non-NIL, then the VIR arc is taken and the item is removed from the HOLD list.

3.6 Useful Actions

3.6.1 Actions which Test the Current Word

A number of functions are provided for testing the current word. These are typically used as further conditions on an arc, as is the CAT function used in the following arc:

    (PUSH pp (CAT prep) ..... (TO s:end))

or as a condition in one of the actions in an arc:

    (CAT det T (and (GETF question)(LIFTR type 'q)) ...)

WRD compares the current word

    (WRD '<word(s)>)
     eg: (WRD who)
        (WRD (which that who))

The WRD function returns T if the current word (i.e. *) matches its single argument. If this argument is an atom then the current word must be identical to it. If it is a list of atoms, then the current word must be a member of this list.

CAT checks the lexical category of the current word

    (CAT '<category>)
     eg: (CAT pro)
        (CAT (n pro npr))

The CAT function tests the current word to see if it can be a member of the lexical category <category>. As with the WRD function, the argument can be an atomic category name or a list of atomic category names.

ROOT checks the root form of the current word

    (ROOT '<root(s)>)
    (ROOT '<root(s)> '<category>)
     eg: (ROOT be)
        (ROOT (be have))

The ROOT function compares the root form of the current word to its argument. Again, the argument can be an atom or a list of atoms. It returns T if and only if the current word has one of the specified root forms. Thus the expression (ROOT be) would be true if the current word

were be, is, am, are, was, etc. Note that if the current word is homo-
morphic between two words with different root forms, both possibilities
will be explored. Thus, if the current word were LIE, both (ROOT lay)
and (ROOT lie) would be true.

The ROOT function takes an optional second argument which can be used
to limit the lexical categories that are considered in determining the
root form of the current word.

GETF gets an inflectional feature

(GETF '<feature name>)
 eg: (GETF tense)

GETF returns the value associated with the feature <feature name> for
the current word. If the current word has no such feature, then NIL is
returned. These features come from three sources:

1. Features on the dictionary entry for the current word.

    For example, the tense and number features for the word IS
    are coded as:

    >   (IS (BE (tense present)(number 3sg))

2. Features generated by the Dictionary Manager.

    For regularly inflected words, certain features are auto-
    matically generated.

3. The FEATURES property of the word.

    Each word can have a FEATURES property associated with it.
    For example, the word GIVE might have the features property:

    >   (TRANSITIVE INDIRECTOBJECT PASSIVE)

    where these features might mean that GIVE is a transitive
    verb which can take an indirect object and can be used in
    a passive sentence.

In cases one and two above, a feature can be:

o   A tuple whose first element is the name of the feature and whose
    second is the value.

o   A list of just the feature name. The value of this feature is
    taken as T.

o   An atomic feature name. The value is assumed to be T.

3.6.2 Actions which Test Arbitrary Words

<u>CHECKF</u> <u>checks</u> <u>an</u> <u>inflectional</u> <u>feature</u>

(CHECKF '<feature> <word> '<cat>)

The CHECKF function is analogous to GETF, differing only in that it applies to an arbitrary word given as its argument. CHECKF returns the value of the feature <feature> associated with the word <word>. An optional third argument, <cat>, determines the lexical category assumed for the word. Thus:

    (CHECKF transitive (GETR verb) 'v)

returns the value of the TRANSITIVE feature for the word in the VERB register when it is interpreted as a verb. Similarly,

    (CHECKF tns * 'v)

returns the TNS feature for the current input word when interpreted as a verb.

3.6.3 Miscellaneous Actions

The BUILDQ function provides a convenient method for constructing arbitrary trees which contain values held in registers. It is modeled after the function described in [Woods71], its syntax being:

    (BUILDQ '<structure> . '<fillers>)

The first argument, <structure>, is an arbitrary list structure which can contain special symbols at its leaves. The function returns a similar structure by replacing these symbols by values computed from the remaining elements, <fillers>.

In filling the structure, BUILDQ traverses the structure in "preorder". If the symbol "+" is encountered, then the next filler argument is taken as the name of an ATN register and its contents are substituted for the "+". If the symbol "*" is encountered, it is replaced by the current value of the atom "*". On encountering the symbol "#", the next filler argument is evaluated and the resulting value used to replace the "#". If the symbol "@" is found as the first element of a list, then the remaining elements of that list are interpreted as above and the results are APPENDed together.

A few examples may make the operation of BUILDQ clear. Suppose we have the following register context:

```
DET             the
NOUN            man
PRE-MODIFIERS   (large heavy)
POST-MODIFIERS  ((PP (in the park)))
```

Then if we evaluate:

```
(BUILDQ (NP # (N +) (DET +)) (gensym) noun det)
```

we would get:

```
(NP GOO27 (N man) (DET the))
```

Evaluating the expression:

```
(BUILDQ (NP # (N +) ( @  (MOD) + +))
        (gensym) noun pre-modifiers post-modifiers)
```

would yield the expression:

```
(NP (N man)
    (MOD large heavy (PP (in the park))))
```

(NEXTWRD) (NEXTWRDS)

The NEXTWRD function returns the next word in the input stream (i.e. the CAR of STRING). Note that this function does not invoke any of the Dictionary Manager Specialists such as the compound word recognizer or the word substituter (see section 5.3) but simply returns CAR of STRING. If there are no more words in the input stream, i.e. STRING is NIL, then NEXTWRD returns NIL.

The NEXTWRDS function returns a list of the possible next words in the input stream after all of the dictionary specialists have been applied.

3.7 Tracing Facilities

Every programming language should provide adequate debugging tools to enable the user to perfect his programs. Since the ATN should be viewed as a kind of programming language, we have provided powerful tracing facilities which we have found to be useful and necessary to build and debug large grammars.

Functions are provided which will print a trace of the developing parse and allow the user to specify arbitrary points at which to suspend computation and enter a "break point". A facility is also provided by which the user can monitor the values being assigned to particular registers.

TRACE-STATE traces ATN states

The function TRACE-STATE allows the user to trace the flow of control thru specified states and optionally break upon entering them. If a state is being traced, the message:

    in state <state name>

will be displayed on the terminal when the state is entered. If the state fails, i.e. no arcs from the state lead to a final state, the following message will be displayed:

    failing from state <state name>

If the user associates a BREAKPOINT with a state, then the message:

    ;BKPT <state name>

will be typed, computation suspended, and a LISP breakpoint entered. Typing an "$P" will resume the ATN computation.

The syntax of the TRACE-STATE function is:

    (TRACE-STATE '<arg1> '<arg2> ... '<argn>)

where each argument specifies one or more states to be traced and optionally associated with a breakpoint. The arguments are interpreted as follows:

<state name>	:	trace the named state
*	:	trace all states
(<state name> BREAK <test>)	:	trace the state and enter a breakpoint if <test> is true.
(* BREAK <test>)	:	trace all states and enter a breakpoint if <test> is true.

UNTRACE untraces ATN states

The function UNTRACE-STATE removes states from the set of ATN states to be traced. Its syntax is:

```
(UNTRACE-STATE '<arg1> ... '<argn>)
```

where each argument specifies one or more states to be "untraced". If
an argument is the name of an ATN state being traced, then that state
is removed from the list. The argument * causes all states to be removed
from the list of states to be traced.

Registers can be traced as well

A similar feature allows one to monitor the values assigned to registers. The function TRACE-REG causes a specified ATN register to be "traced". Whenever a value is assigned to that register with a SETR, the
message:

```
setting register <register name> to <value>
```

will be typed on the TTY. Similar messages are displayed when a register is set via the functions LIFTR or SENDR.

The syntax of the function TRACE-REG is similar to that of TRACE-STATE,
being:

```
(TRACE-REG '<arg1> '<arg2> ... '<argn>)
```

An argument can be the name of a register, the special "wildcard" *, or
a three-tuple (<register name> BREAK <test>). The last case allows one
to trace the setting of a register and enter a BREAKPOINT if the arbitrary lisp expression <test> is true.

The function UNTRACE-REG is used to remove specified registers from the
list of registers being traced. Its argument convention is similar to
that of UNTRACE-STATE.

3.8 Global Variables
The following is a list of the most important global variables in the
interpreter.

-   * The current constituent
    The global variable * is always bound to the "current constitu-
    ent. Precisely what this is depends on the context. Within a CAT
    arc, it is bound to the root form of the current word. Within a
    PUSH arc it is bound to the constituent POPped by the sub-compu-
    tation (except in the "preactions" where * is the current word).

In a VIR arc, * is bound to the element being removed from the HOLD list. For the other arc types, it is bound to the current word (i.e. LEX).

In several other contexts, * is temporarily bound to other elements. For example, when evaluating the <test> in a VIR arc or in a (GETR <register> NEAREST <test>), * is bound to the candidate element.

- LEX The current word
  The atom LEX is always bound to the current word, exactly as it appears in the input string. If the input string is exhausted, then LEX is bound to NIL.

- STRING The input string
  The atom STRING is always bound to a list of the words remaining in the input string.

- STACK
  STACK is a list of the names of states PUSHed to which have not POPped. This can be used to determine how deeply embedded the current computation is. For example, the following POP arc will only be taken if we will be returning to the top level and the input is exhausted:

```
(POP (buildnp)
     (AND (NULL stack)(NULL *)(NULL string)))
```

The following additional global variables may be of some use to the user:

- ALIST is an association list which encodes the contents of the registers, both current and past. Elements of ALIST are tuples whose CAR is the name of a register and whose CDR is a value associated with that register.

- STATE is the current ATN state in interpreted grammars. The variable is undefined in compiled grammars.

- ARC is the current arc being taken in interpreted grammars. It is undefined in compiled grammars.

- USE-ALL-WORDS? is a variable which controls the ability to POP to the TOP-LEVEL when words remain in the input string. This is permitted only when USE-ALL-WORDS? is bound to NIL.

- LEXPRESCAN? is a variable which controls when the dictionary manager functions are invoked. If it is bound to T, then the dictionary manager is applied to the entire string before the grammar is applied and the results stored in a chart form. If NIL, then the dictionary manager functions are applied as input is needed.

- ALIST-STACK is stack of the values of ALIST for higher levels of computation.

- ARC-STACK is stack of pending actions on any active PUSH arcs (i.e. those which have not yet been popped to).

- POPSTACK is a stack of tags to the active PUSH arcs.

4.0 THE ATN COMPILER

4.1 Introduction

The purpose of the ATN Compiler is to translate ATN networks into pure LISP code which can be executed directly. This code can subsequently be translated into machine language code by a standard LISP compiler. In fact, the PLANES ATN compiler has been written in such a way as to facilitate the direct compilation of ATN networks into machine language by the MacLISP compiler [Moon74].

Burton describes another compiler for ATN grammars in [Burt76b]. The scope of this compiler is similar to the one described in this section, although the implementational details and some of the capabilities are quite different. Finin describes an ATN compiler written in the APL programming language which is very similar to the PLANES ATN compiler in [FINI78].

Advantages of compilation

The advantages of compiling an ATN network are the same as those of any compilation process: reduced execution time and storage space. We have applied our compiler on a modified version of the LUNAR English grammar [Wood72] and found that the execution time for the resulting LISP code was decreased by about a factor of 2. The resultant machine language code achieved a speed up factor of 5 to 10.

The compiler is able to preserve all of the features available under the interpreter. A grammar writer need take no special steps or consider-

ations if he intends to compile his network. In other words, if one has
a system of ATN networks which behaves correctly in the interpreter,
then compiling these networks without modifications will result in compiled code which also behaves correctly.

The PLANES ATN compiler has the additional feature of being able to incrementally compile ATN grammars. Each state is compiled independantly,
making it easy to use the compiler on a grammar which is still evolving.
Incremental compilation also allows one to replace the compiled version
of a single state with an uncompiled version. Thus, if one discovers a
bug in some state of a large compiled grammar, he can edit the source
code and reload only the corrected state. The rest of the compiled grammar can still be used.

Special Features of the Compiler

A compiled ATN network is more efficient mainly because the interpretation stage is by-passed. This compiler also achieves greater efficiency
thru four additional optimization processes:

1. The resulting LISP code is locally "optimized" by a simple
    pattern matching scheme.

2. Certain common actions and arc conditions are "open coded"
    into more primitive LISP code.

3. The compiler automatically detects local contexts in which
    certain ATN features are not being used (e.g. explicit failure
    via the FAIL function). In these contexts, code to handle these
    features need not be generated.

4. The user is able to globally "turn off" a number of general ATN
    features which he is not using. This causes the compiler not to
    produce the code necessary to implement these features.

4.1.1 Compilation of a State

The basic organization of the ATN compiler is shown in figure 5 (An
Overview of the ATN Compiler). The function COMPILESTATE1 is applied to
each state in the network. It produces a LISP function which will simulate the action of the state when called. In doing so, it applies the
function COMPILEARC to each arc in the state. The resulting code for
each arc is combined with additional code to produce the function.

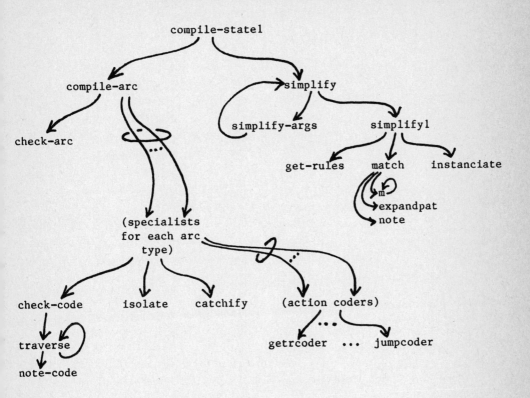

Fig. 5: An Overview of the ATN Compiler

The basic frame for an ATN state function is:

```
(DEFUN (<state name> ATNEXPR ATNSUBR)
       NIL
       <tracing code>
       (CATCH (PROGN <code for arc 1>
                    <code for arc 2>
                    ...)
              <state name> )
       <more tracing code>
       'FAIL)
```

DEFUN is, of course, the MacLisp function defining function. The first argument gives the name of the function being defined (<state name>) and the properties under which its uncompiled and compiled definitions are to be stored (ATNEXPR and ATNSUBR, respectively). The second argument to DEFUN is NIL, indicating that we are defining a function of no arguments.

The (CATCH ... <state name>) construct is included to implement the ability to fail to a named state from a later point. The inclusion of the tracing code and the (CATCH ... <state name>) expression is under the control of the user thru switches described in a later section.

Once this code has been produced, an optimization procedure is applied to the function. The result is then evaluated if we are in the LISP interpreter or passed to the MacLisp compiler if it is resident.

4.1.2 Compilation of an Individual Arc

The function COMPILEARC is responsible for writing an expression for an individual arc. Its job is to:

1. verify that the arc is in a legal format.

2. dispatch the arc to the appropriate specialist for compilation.

The verification includes a simple check on the last action of an arc. For arc types POP, TO, JUMP and DO this action should not specify a destination (i.e. call TO or JUMP). For the rest of the arc types, the terminal arc should be a destination. If this condition is not met a warning message is displayed.

Each arc compiler specialist compiles one type of arc. It examines the condition and actions and produces a LISP expression which simulates that arc. The general form of the code for an arc is given below:

```
(CATCH ((LAMBDA (ALIST) (AND <arc dependent code>
                            <test>
                            (PROGN . <actions>)))
        ALIST)
       ARCFAILURE)
```

The (CATCH ... ARCFAILURE) construction is necessary to handle a possible (FAIL 'ARC) in the <actions> or the <test>. The ((LAMBDA (ALIST) ...) ALIST) is required to isolate the possible side effects caused by the arc.

Before adding these two fragments, the arc compiler checks to see if they are really necessary. The <test> and <actions> are examined to see if they might contain a call to a function with a side effect (e.g. a call to SETR) or a call to the FAIL function. In examining the expressions, the compiler must be aware of which expressions are "executable" and which are potentially "data".

The following conservative algorithm is used to determine whether evaluating an s-expression will generate a side effect.

1. Trivial case
    Atoms, of course, can't cause side effects. Return NIL.

2. Known offenders
    Some functions are known to cause side effects (e.g. SETR).
    Return T.

3. Guilty until proven innocent
    If the function is unknown (i.e. one which the user has written)
    then assume it might generate a side effect. Return T.

4. Fexpers, etc.
    If the function has no arguments or is known not to evaluate
    any of its arguments, then return NIL.

5. Recurse
    Recursively apply this procedure to those arguments of the s-expression which are evaluated. If any generates a side effect, then return T, else return NIL. Here the compiler must know how

a function evaluates its arguments. For the standard built-in
LISP functions and the built-in ATN functions and actions this
information is stored for each function in an "evaluation tem-
plate".

An analogous procedure is used to determine if evaluating an expression
might generate a failure. If the arc contains no expressions which might
have a side effect then the LAMBDA expression is omitted. If no FAIL action is found, then the CATCH is omitted.

Another of the compiler's optimizing technique is to delay the CATCH
(if any) and LAMBDA binding (if any) until the last possible moment.
Thus, the following WRD arc:

```
(WRD because (getr obj)(setr conj *)(to s:conjoined))
```

is compiled as:

```
(AND (EQ * 'because)
     (GETR obj)
     ((LAMBDA (ALIST) (SETR conj *)(TO s:conjoined))
      ALIST))
```

Note that the LAMBDA binding is done only if the arc is actually taken
and that no CATCH was generated since no FAIL action was contained in
the arc.

4.1.3 Optimization

The optimization phase of the compiler was originally added to make the
compiler easier to write and debug. The idea was to simplify the code
generation process for each of the arcs. In compiling an arc, we needn't
produce efficient code, but merely straightforward code which is guaranteed to work properly. Once the code has been generated, a standard "optimizing" routine is applied to it to simplify the expression.

The General Procedure

The basic procedure to optimize a LISP s-expression it to traverse the
expression in "post order", applying a simplification algorithm at each
node. Thus the expression is optimized "from the bottom up", i.e. the
arguments to a function are optimized before the function call itself
is optimized. We must take care, however, that the optimization proce-

dure is only applied to "executable" nodes and not to "data nodes". An "executable" node is one which is <u>known</u> to be evaluated as a LISP expression. All other nodes are assumed to be "data" nodes.

Thus, the optimizer does not attempt to optimize a function call unless that function is:

o known to be a EXPR, SUBR, LEXPR or LSUBR

o known to be a FEXPR or FSUBR which evaluates all of its
   arguments (e.g. AND, OR, etc.)

o a special FEXPR or FSUBR that the optimizer "understands".

The functions covered in the third case are those which are known to evaluate some of these arguments in a special manner. For example, the optimizer knows that the function PROG evaluates all but its first argument and that the arguments to the COND function are lists of expressions to be optimized.

<u>Simplification</u>

Once the arguments to a function have been optimized, the function call is <u>simplified</u>. This simplification is driven by a set of production-like rules which specify code transformations. These transformations simplify the code but do not change its behavior. These rules are three-tuples which have the form:

    (<pattern> <result> <restrictions>)

Each rule states that if a LISP expression matches <pattern> and <restrictions> evaluates to non-NIL, then it can always be replaced by the simpler s-expression <result>.

The <pattern> and <result> elements of a rule are general s-expressions in which the characters * and ? have special significance. The atom "?" is allowed to match any single s-expression. The atom "*" may match zero or more sister s-expressions. Any atom whose first character is a "?" or a "*" behaves in a similar manner except that that atom is bound to the s-expression(s) matched. As an example, consider the pattern:

    (PROG ?A *B (RETURN *))

when matched against the following expression:

```
(PROG (A B C)
      (SETQ A (TIMES X X))
      (SETQ B (TIMES X A))
      (RETURN (LIST A B)))
```

The match succeeds and has the side effects of setting the variables ?A and *B to (A B C) and ((SETQ A (TIMES X X))(SETQ B (TIMES X A))), respectively. Figure 6 (Some Simplification Rules) gives a list of some of the simplification rules used in the ATN compiler.

Application of the simplification rules

The simplification rules are applied according to the following algorithm:

1. Collect the rules which may apply.
    The rules are indexed by function name (i.e. the CAR of the expression).

2. Find a rule which matches the expression.
    The matcher compares the <pattern> and <restriction> of each rule against the data until a match is found.

3. If no matching rule was found, then stop else continue.

4. Replace the expression.
    Replace the expression with the instantiation of the <result> element of the rule found in step 2.

5. Continue with step 1.
    Since the function being called may have changed, we must start from the top.

Figure 7 (An Example of Simplification) shows an example of the simplification process.

4.2 Using the ATN Compiler

The ATN compiler can easily be used to produce executable LISP code in the LISP interpreter or to produce machine language code in conjunction with the standard MacLisp compiler. In either case, the user can selectively disable unused features to achieve faster execution time. This is discussed in section 4.3.3.

```
(AND)                           NIL
(AND *A T *B)                   (AND *A *B)                    (OR *A *B)
(AND ?A)                        ?A
(AND *A (AND *B) *C)            (AND *A *B *C)


(APPEND *A (LIST *B)(LIST *C) *D)  (APPEND *A (LIST *B *C) *D)


(CAR (CAR ?A))                  (CAAR ?A)
 ...etc...


(COND)                          NIL
(COND *A (NIL *) *B)            (COND *A *B))
(COND *A (T *B) *C)             (COND *A (T *B))               *C
(COND (?A ?B))                  (AND ?A ?B)
(COND (T *A))                   (PROGN *A)
(COND (?A))                     ?A
(COND *E (?A *B (PROGN *C) *D) *F) (COND *E (?A *B *C *D) *F)))


(CONS ?A NIL)                   (NCONS ?A)


(DEFUN ?A ?B *C (PROGN *D) *E)  (DEFUN ?A ?B *C *D *E)
(DEFUN ?A ?B *C NIL *D)         (DEFUN ?A ?B *C *D)


(DO ?A ?B *C (PROGN *D) *E)     (DO ?A ?B *C *D *E)


(EQ ?A NIL)                     (NULL ?A)


(EQUAL '?A ?B)                  (EQ '?A ?B)                    (ATOM ?A)
(EQUAL ?A '?B)                  (EQ ?A '?B)           .        (ATOM ?B)


(LAMBDA ?A *B (PROGN *C) *D)    (LAMBDA ?A *B *C *D)


(LIST ?A)                       (NCONS ?A)


(PROG ?A *B (PROGN *C) *D)      (PROG ?A *B *C *D)


(PROGN ?A)                      ?A
(PROGN *A (PROGN *B) *C)        (PROGN *A *B *C)


(OR)                            NIL
(OR ?A)                         ?A
(OR *A T *)                     (OR *A)
(OR *A NIL *B)                  (OR *A *B)
```


        Fig. 6: Some Simplification Rules

```
(PROGN (AND T (COND ((> X 10.)(SETQ X 10.)))))

              |_(cond (?a ?b))  ==>  (and ?a ?b)


(PROGN (AND T (AND (> X 10.)(SETQ X 10.)))))

      |_(and *a (and *b) *c)  ==>  (and *a *b *c)



(PROGN (AND T (> X 10.)(SETQ X 10.)))

      |_(and *a t *b)  ==>  (and *a *b)


(PROGN (AND (> X 10.)(SETQ X 10.)))
|_(progn ?a)  ==>  ?a


(AND (> X 10.)(SETQ X 10.))
```

Fig. 7: An Example of Simplification

4.2.1 Compiling Networks into LISP Code

This section describes how one can compile networks into LISP code given
he has a LISP into which the ATN interpreter has been loaded and the networks defined. Once the ATN compiler has been loaded, the user can then
set whatever switches he wants (using SETQ). A single ATN state can be
compiled with the function COMPILESTATE. This function takes one (unevaluated) argument, the name of the ATN state to be compiled. The function defines an equivalent function which will be called whenever control is transferred to that ATN state.

The function COMPILEATN can be used to compile an entire ATN network.
Its single (unevaluated) argument should be the name of the ATN network
to be compiled. It simply applies COMPILESTATE to each of the states
found in the network.

4.2.2 Compilation in the Lisp Compiler

To compile a file of ATN networks with the standard MacLisp compiler one
need only ensure that the ATN compiler is loaded into the MacLisp compiler. The easiest way to do this is to include the following expression
at the top of the file containing an ATN grammar.

```
(DECLARE (FASLOAD ATNCOMPILER ... ))
```

This will cause the ATN compiler to be automatically loaded when the
file is compiled. In the environment of the compiler, the functions
DEFARC, DEFSTATE, DEFINTERUPT, etc. are defined to be macros compile
their arguments into Lisp code. Thus, the Lisp compiler sees only the
Lisp code and not the grammar in the ATN formalism.

Switches may be set in a similar manner. For example, one might include
the expression:

```
(DECLARE (FASLOAD ATNCOMPILER ...)
         (SETQ ATNTRACE? NIL)       ;no tracing
         (SETQ FAILARC? NIL))       ;no (FAIL 'ARC) actions
```

in the file containing the networks.

Interactions with NCOMPLR

If the ATN networks call any user defined functions they may have to be
declared to NCOMPLR. Auxiliary functions must be declared if they are

FEXPRs, FSUBRs, LEXPRs, LSUBRs, or MACROs. For an explanation of how to do this, consult [Moon74].

4.2.3 Switches

The following switches control the generation of code by the ATN compiler. For each switch the default value is given after its name.

[1] ATNTRACE?   T

If ATNTRACE? is T then code which allows states to be traced (i.e. via TRACE-STATE) will be generated. A NIL value supresses the generation of this code. Thus, this switch might be set to NIL if the network is fully debugged or a production module is desired.

[2] ATNFAILARC?   T

If ATNFAILARC? is T then code will be generated which allows one to use the (FAIL 'ARC) action. If NIL, then this code is not generated.

[3] ATNFAILSTATE?   T

Code which allows one to fail to a named state is generated if this switch is T. If NIL, then the code is not generated. Recall that one can fail to a named state with the FAIL arc or the FAIL action.

[4] ATNFAILPUSH?   T

If T, then code will be generated which allows one to fail from a sub-computation (i.e. to the last PUSH arc or PUSHATN action). If NIL, then the code will not be generated.

[5] ATNFAIL?   T

This switch has no effect if it has the value T, but a NIL value disables all explicit failure. Thus, if ATNFAIL? is NIL, this implies that ATNFAILARC = ATNFAILSTATE = ATNFAILPUSH = NIL.

[6] ATNSIMPLECAT?   NIL

This switch controls the code generated for a CAT arc and the CAT action. If it is T, then it is assumed that each word will have at most one entry for a particular lexical category in the dictionary. If this is so, the compiler need not set up a decision point for each CAT arc or action.

5.0   THE LEXICON

5.1   Introduction

The lexicon consists of two parts: the DICTIONARY which contains words and certain features associated with them and the DICTIONARY MANAGER which is a package of procedures for accessing, maintaining, and updating the dictionary.

A dictionary entry for a word typically consists of the syntactic category that the word belongs to and a list of syntactic features for the word when interpreted under that category. In English, as in many languages, a word can belong to several lexical categories. In such cases, multiple entries can be made in the Dictionary. For example the word CRASH might have the following entries:

```
    CRASH      N -es
    CRASH      V -es-ed (intransitive)
```

This says that crash can be interpreted as a noun (N) whose plural is formed be adding the suffix "es" or as an intransitive verb (V) whose inflectional forms can be generated by adding the suffixes "es" or "ed".

Initially, no entries need exist for the regularly inflected forms of words. Such forms are discovered and entries for them generated as they are needed. For example, if the input contains the word CRASHED, a set of programs (Morphology Specialists) are invoked which discover that CRASHED is the past tense form of the root word CRASH. These programs insert the lexical entry:

```
    CRASHED    V (CRASH) (tense past)(intransitive)
```

The words CRASHES and CRASHING are similarly recognized and their lexical entries generated.

5.2   The Dictionary Format

The dictionary entry for a word is stored on the LISP property list for that atom (i.e. the word). The standard property names which might be used are atoms representing lexical categories (e.g. N for noun, DET for determiner, etc.), and three special atoms: COMPOUNDS, SUBSTITUTE, and FEATURES.

For each lexical category, <C>, a word might have a property indexed under the indicator <C>. The value of this property depends on the particular category and the relationship between the word and its root form. These are discussed in the next section.

The value of the COMPOUNDS property for a word is a tree which represents pre-defined compound phrases which that word may start. Associated with each phrase in the tree is a word which that phrase should be mapped into. The user need not concern himself with the exact representation of this tree as the functions DEFPHRASE and DEFP (described later) can be used to create it.

The value of the SUBSTITUTE property for a word is a list of phrases which should replace that word. Thus, it forms a kind of inverse to the COMPOUNDS mechanism. This property is discussed further under the functions DEFSUBSTITUTE and DEFSUB.

The value of the FEATURES property is a list of atoms or sublists which name "features" to be associated with the word. These features may be accessed in several ways within the ATN interpreter (see, for example, the functions GETF and CHECKF).

The value of a lexical category property for a word specifies the root form(s) of the word and a set of inflectional features to be associated with the word. The exact encoding of this information is as follows:

1. If the value is a list whose first element is atomic, then the first element is the root form of the word and the remaining elements are the inflectional features. For example:

   BLEW V (blow (tns past))

   says that the word BLEW is the past tense of the verb BLOW.

2. If the value is a list whose first element is a sub-list, then the word has more than one possible root form when interpreted under this lexical category. Each sub-list should be of the form discussed in point one above. AN example is:

   SAW V ((see (tns past))
           ((saw (tns present)(untensed))))

   This property states that the word SAW is either the past tense form of the verb SEE or the present/untensed form of the verb SAW (what we do to a board).

3. If the value is atomic, then the word itself is taken as the root form and the inflectional features are supplied by the dictionary manager. Exactly what features are supplied is described in the next section. Some examples are:

```
COOK V s-ed
     N -s
FAST ADJ er-est
     V   s-ed
     N   -s
```

The meaning of atomic category values

The lexical categories N (noun), V (verb), ADJ (adjective), and ADV (adverb) are treated in a special manner by the dictionary manager. An atomic value for one of these properties can specify that the word fits one of a number of regularly inflected paradigms. For nouns, the following possibilities exist:

* *   The noun is irregular.
* -s   The plural is formed by adding an "s".
* -es The plural is formed by adding an "es" or, if the noun ends in a "y", by deleting the "y" and adding an "ies".

For verbs, we have the following:

* *   The verb is irregular.
* s-ed   The third person singular is formed by adding an "s" and the past/past-participle is formed by adding an "ed".
* es-ed The third person singular is formed by adding an "es" and the past/past-participle is formed by adding an "ed".

For adjectives (ADJ) and adverbs (ADV) we have the following possibilities:

* *   The word has no regularly inflected comparative or superlative (e.g. UNSUCCESSFUL).
* er-est The comparative and superlative are formed by adding an ER and EST, respectively (e.g. LONG). If the word ends in a Y, then it is first changed to an I (e.g. HAPPY).
* r-st   Add an R or ST to form the comparative and superlative (e.g. WIDE).

5.3 The Dictionary Manager

The Dictionary Manager is a collection of programs which access, maintain, and update the Dictionary. They also act as a filter between the

Parser and the user's input suggesting alternative words as the 'next word'. As each word of the input is needed by the parser, the Dictionary Manager checks to see if there is an entry in the Dictionary for that word or if the word belongs to certain categories which are recognized procedurally, such as numbers. If an entry exists, then the word is passed on to the parser with a list of features associated with the word. These features are those found in the dictionary together with any others suggested by the Morphology Specialists.

If the word does not have a lexical entry, then a series of Morphology Specialists are invoked to see if the word is a regularly inflected form of a known word. These specialists use their knowledge of typical English affixes to propose candidate 'roots' for the word. Each candidate is then looked up in the Dictionary and, if found, checked to see if it accepts the affix removed.

If this process fails then the Punctuation Checker is called which examines the word to see if it might contain any embedded punctuation. For example, if the input is TAIL-NUMBER, the Punctuation Checker would suggest that the two words TAIL and NUMBER be substituted.

Finally, if the word is still unknown, control is passed to the New Word Learner. This module interacts with the user and attempts to create a lexical entry for the word.

Two other subsystems generate alternative suggestions for the 'next word': a Compound Word Recognizer and a Word Substituter. The Compound Word Recognizer is used to map short phrases into single "words". For example, we might map the phrases UNITED STATES and UNITED STATES OF AMERICA into the single "word" USA. Just before a new word is passed to the parser, the Compound Word Recognizer checks to see if that word can begin a phrase that it knows. If so, then it checks the rest of the sentence, and if it matches, suggests the alternative 'next word'.

The Word Substituter provides a similar mechanism - one which can expand a single word in the input into a sequence words. For example, the word DIDN'T could be expanded into the sequence DID NOT. The sequence of words substituted can be of zero length, which provides a facility for ignoring words. This facility might be used, for example, to ignore extraneous punctuation.

5.4 Auxiliary Functions

Several functions are provided which simplify creating dictionary entries and loading and manipulating dictionary files.

DEFINEWORD and DEFW create dictionary entries for a word

(DEFINEWORD <word> <definition>)
(DEFW '<word> . '<definition>)

These functions are used to create a dictionary entry for the word <word> or to add information to the dictionary entry for <word> if an entry is already in the dictionary.

The function DEFINEWORD takes two arguments: a word and a "property list fragment". It adds the property list fragment to the property list of the word.

The function DEFW takes an indefinite number of arguments, none of which are evaluated. The first is the word and the remaining ones are alternating property names and values. The name-value pairs are added to the word's property list.

Examples of these functions in use are:

(DEFINEWORD 'fly '(v * n -es features (intrans trans)))
(DEFINEWORD 'i '(pro *))
(DEFW ship n -s v -s-ed features (trans passive))
(DEFW ? punct *)

DEFINEPHRASE and DEFP Create Compounds properties

(DEFINEPHRASE <phrase> <word>)
(DEFP '<phrase> '<word>)

These functions create COMPOUNDS entries for a word. A COMPOUNDS entry will cause the ATN interpreter to map a sequence of words in the input string into a single word. These functions will cause the input sequence <phrase> (which should be a list of atoms) to be replaced by the single word <word>. For example:

(DEFP (how much) howmuch)

would create or modify the COMPOUNDS entry for the word HOW such that if the ATN interpreter encounters the two word sequence "HOW MUCH" in the input string, it will replace these two words with the single word HOWMUCH. Note that if subsequent parsing fails, the interpreter will also try parsing the string as containing the two individual words HOW and MUCH.

Several COMPOUNDS entries can be created at once by including sub-lists in the first argument. For example,

    (DEFP (how (much many)) howmuch)

is equivalent to:

    (DEFP (how much) howmuch)
    (DEFP (how many) howmuch)

Thus, a sublist in the <phrase> argument specifies that one of its elements be in the compound phrase.

DEFSUBSTITUTE and DEFSUB create SUBSTITUTE entries

(DEFSUBSTITUTE <word> <phrase>)
(DEFSUB '<word> '<phrase>)

These functions create or modify SUBSTITUTE properties for a word. The first argument is an atom and the second argument is an atom or list of atoms which should be substituted for the first whenever it occurs in the input string. The following example will explain the various possibilities:

- (DEFSUB aircraft plane)
  If the second argument is an atom (but not the atom NIL), then it will replace the first argument in the input string. Thus, PLANE will replace instances of the word AIRCRAFT in the input string.

- (DEFSUB don't (do not))
  If the second argument is a list of atoms, then that list will replace the first argument in the input string. Thus, occurances of the word DON'T will be replaced by the two words DO and NOT.

- (DEFSUB please NIL)
  If the second argument is NIL, then the first argument will be deleted from the input string. Thus instances of the word PLEASE will be deleted from the input string. This provides a simple method for ignoring certain words (such as "extraneous" punctuation).

As with the COMPOUNDS mechanism, if a substitution is made and failure later backs up to that point, the ATN interpreter will attempt to continue the parse without making the substitution.

Dictionary Files

If one is dealing with a large number of words it is convenient to store them in a file in a special simplified format. Two functions are provided to manipulate such dictionary files.

The format of a dictionary file is a sequence of lists. The first element of each list is an atom or a list. If it is an atom, then the list is taken as the argument list to the function DEFW. In other words, the first element is a word and the remaining elements are alternating property-names and associated values. If the first element is a sub-list, then the entire list is used to supply arguments to the function DEFP. In this case, the first element is a phrase and the remaining element (there should be only one) is the word that the phrase gets mapped into. The following might be the beginning of such a dictionary file:

```
(a det *)
(about prep *)
(an det *)
((and / or) and-or)
(and-or conj *)
(ask v s-ed features (trans indobj thatcomp tocomp))
    .
    .
    .
```

LOADDIC loads a Dictionary File

(LOADDIC . '<file specifications>)
eg: (LOADDIC navy dic ...)

The function LOADDIC is used to read a dictionary file and create the specified entries. Its syntax is similar to that for the MacLISP I/O functions ("old I/O" functions, that is). It takes from one to four arguments where the first is the file name, the second the file extension, the third the device and the fourth is the PPN. Unsupplied arguments are defaulted as follows:

```
arg 1 :   <file name>       :  must be supplied
arg 2 :   <file extension>  :  defaults to DIC
arg 3 :   <device>          :  defaults to current device
arg 4 :   <ppn>             :  defaults to the current ppn
```

GRINDDIC reformats a dictionary file

```
(GRINDDIC . '<file specifications>)
eg: (GRINDDIC navy dic)
```

This function sorts and grinds (i.e. pretty-prints) a dictionary file. The sorting function sorts each top level list in the file by the "left-most" atom in the list only. The argument syntax and meaning is identical to the function LOADDIC. The function GRINDDIC is useful in maintaining growing dictionaries in an easily readable format.

Miscellaneous dictionary managing functions are provided

Currently, one other auxiliary function is supplied for managing a dictionary. The function SHOWWORD "pretty-prints" the dictionary entry for a word. It's syntax is:

```
(SHOWWORD '<word>)
```

6.0 AUXILIARY FUNCTIONS

6.1 Interfacing with the LISP Editor

The functions EDITATN and EDITSTATE allow one to apply a general purpose List structure editor [Gabr75] to ATN networks and individual states. These functions do not normally reside in the ATN system but are automatically loaded if they are called. In addition, this subsystem modifies appropriate Editor variables so that the editor can recognize ATN network definitions in files. Thus, one can say (EDIT <network name> <file specifications>) and expect the editor to find the network definition in the specified file. This also allows one to use the REFILE editor command to update the file once the networks have been edited. A special purpose ATN Grammar editor called NETEDI is also available. This editor is described in [Fini77b].

EDITATN applies the Editor to an ATN network

This function sets up an ATN network for editing and then invokes the LISP Editor. It takes one or no arguments, the syntax being:

    (EDITATN <network name>)
    (EDITATN <state name>)
    (EDITATN *)
    (EDITATN)

If EDITATN is called with the name of a network, then that network is set up for editing. If called with the name of an individual state, then the editor is invoked on the network which includes that state. If called with the argument *, then the network which includes the current state is edited. If no argument is given, then the network which was last edited is set up for re-editing.

EDITSTATE invokes the editor on an individual ATN state

The function EDITSTATE is similar to EDITATN expect that it applies the editor to an individual ATN state. If an argument is given, it can be the name of the state to be edited or the special atom * which refers to the state that the interpreter is currently in. If no argument is given, the editor is primed with the last edited ATN state. The syntax is:

    (EDITSTATE '<state name>)
    (EDITSTATE *)
    (EDITSTATE)

6.2 Displaying ATN Networks and States

SHOWATN displays an ATN network

The function SHOWATN is used to display an entire ATN network in "pretty print" format. The optional argument is interpreted in a manner identical to that for the function EDITATN. The options are:

    (SHOWATN '<network name>)
    (SHOWATN '<state name>)
    (SHOWATN *)
    (SHOWATN)

SHOWSTATE displays an individual ATN state

The SHOWSTATE function "pretty prints" an individual ATN state. Its optional argument is interpreted like that of EDITSTATE. The syntax is:

```
(SHOWSTATE '<state name>)
(SHOWSTATE  )
(SHOWSTATE)
```

7.O EXAMPLES

7.1 A Sample ATN Network

The following three ATN networks comprise a simple grammar to a small subset of English. Note that most features of English syntax are not handled. Two auxiliary functions, BUILDSENTENCE and BUILDNP, are used to construct the parse trees.

```
(defatn sentence
    ((s: (cat aux t (setr v *) (to s:aux))
         (push np: t (setr subj *) (to s:subj))
         (vir np t (setr subj *) (to s:subj)))
     (s:aux (push np: t (setr subj *) (to s:v)))
     (s:subj (cat v t (setr v *) (to s:v)))
     (s:v (cat v
                (getf pastpart)
                (cond ((eq $v 'be)
                       (hold $subj 'np nil)
                       (setr subj 'someone))
                      ((eq $v 'have)
                       (setr aspect 'perfect))
                      (t (fail 'arc)))
                (setr v *)
                (to s:v))
          (push np: (getf transative $v) (setr obj *) (to s:obj))
          (vir np (getf transative $v) (setr obj *) (to s:obj))
          (and (wrd to (getf strans $v))
               (push s:subj
                     t
                     (sendr subj $obj)
                     (setr obj *)
                     (to s:end)))
          (and (wrd that (getf strans $v))
               (push s: t (setr obj *) (to s:end)))
```

```
             (jump s:end (getf intrans $v)))
      (s:obj (push np:
                   (getf indobj $v)
                   (setr indobj $obj)
                   (setr obj *)
                   (to s:end))
             (vir np
                   (getf indobj $v)
                   (setr indobj $obj)
                   (setr obj *)
                   (to s:end))
             (and (wrd to)
                  (push s:subj
                        t
                        (sendr subj $obj)
                        (setr obj *)
                        (to s:end)))
             (jump s:end))
      (s:end (push pp: (cat prep) (addr pps *))
             (pop (buildsentence)))))


(defatn noun-phrase
    ((np: (cat det t (setr det *) (to np:det)) (jump np:det))
     (np:det (cat adj t (addr adj *) (to np:det))
             (cat n t (addr adj *) (to np:det))
             (cat n t (setr n *) (to np:n)))
     (np:n (push pp: (cat prep) (addr modifiers *) (to np:n))
           (and (wrd (which who that whom)
                     t
                     (hold (buildnp) 'np nil))
                (push s: t (addr modifiers *) (to np:end)))
           (jump np:end))
     (np:end (pop (buildnp)))))


(defatn prep-phrase
    ((pp: (cat prep t (setr prep *) (to pp:prep)))
     (pp:prep (push np: t (setr np *) (to pp:end))
              (vir np t (setr np *) (to pp:end)))
     (pp:end (pop (buildq (pp + +) prep np)))))
```

```
(defun buildsentence nil
    (buildq (s (verb +) (subj +) (obj +) (indobj +) (pps +))
            v
            subj
            obj
            indobj
            pps))

(defun buildnp nil
    (buildq (np (n +) (det +) (@ (adj) +) (@ (modifiers) +))
            n
            det
            adj
            modifiers))
```

7.2 A Sample Dictionary

This example shows a small dictionary which was used with the example
network to parse the sentences in this appendix. Only the lexical features used by the simple grammar are included for these words.

```
(a det *)
(aircraft substitute ((plane)))
(by prep *)
(electrical adj *)
(engine n -s)
(extensive adj *)
(for prep *)
(good adj *)
(has v (have (tns present)))
(have v irr features (transative))
(I n *)
(in prep *)
(list n -s v s-ed features (transative))
(maintenance n -s)
(me n (i))
(of prep *)
(plane n -s)
(poor adj er-est)
(record n -s)
(repair n -s v s-ed features (transative))
(require v s-d features (transative))
(see v irr features (transative intransative))
```

```
(show v s-ed features (transative indobj))
(that det *)
(the det *)
(to prep *)
(very adj *)
(want v s-ed n -s features (transative indobj strans))
(were v (be (tns past)))
(which det *)
(which det *)
(you n *)
(? substitute (nil))
(/. substitute (nil))
```

7.3 Examples of Operation

Given below are the results of applying the example ATN network to six sentences. For each, the sentence is given exactly as it was typed, preceded by a ">>". Following that, the list POPed by the ATN network is given.

>> which planes required engine maintenance?

```
(S (VERB REQUIRE)
   (SUBJ (NP (N PLANE) (DET WHICH) (ADJ) (MODIFIERS)))
   (OBJ (NP (N MAINTENANCE) (DET NIL) (ADJ ENGINE) (MODIFIERS)))
   (INDOBJ NIL)
   (PPS NIL))
```

>> electrical repairs were required.

```
(S (VERB REQUIRE)
   (SUBJ SOMEONE)
   (OBJ (NP (N REPAIR) (DET NIL) (ADJ ELECTRICAL) (MODIFIERS)))
   (INDOBJ NIL)
   (PPS NIL))
```

>> I want a list of those planes

```
(S (VERB WANT)
   (SUBJ (NP (N  I) (DET NIL) (ADJ) (MODIFIERS)))
   (OBJ (NP (N PLANE) (DET THOSE) (ADJ) (MODIFIERS)))
   (INDOBJ (NP (N YOU)
               (DET NIL)
               (ADJ)
```

```
                      (MODIFIERS (PP TO
                                  (NP (N LIST)
                                      (DET NIL)
                                      (ADJ)
                                      (MODIFIERS))))))))
       (PPS NIL))
```

>> I want you to list those planes.

```
(S (VERB WANT)
   (SUBJ (NP (N I) (DET NIL) (ADJ) (MODIFIERS)))
   (OBJ (S (VERB LIST)
           (SUBJ (NP (N YOU) (DET NIL) (ADJ) (MODIFIERS)))
           (OBJ (NP (N PLANE) (DET THOSE) (ADJ) (MODIFIERS)))
           (INDOBJ NIL)
           (PPS NIL)))
   (INDOBJ NIL)
   (PPS NIL))
```

>> I want to see a list of the planes that required
   extensive engine repairs.

```
(S
 (VERB WANT)
 (SUBJ (NP (N I) (DET NIL) (ADJ) (MODIFIERS)))
 (OBJ
  (S (VERB SEE)
     (SUBJ (NP (N I) (DET NIL) (ADJ) (MODIFIERS)))
     (OBJ (NP (N LIST)
              (DET A)
              (ADJ)
              (MODIFIERS (PP OF
                            (NP (N PLANE)
                                (DET THE)
                                (ADJ)
                                (MODIFIERS (S (VERB REQUIRE)
                                              (SUBJ (NP (N PLANE)
                                                        (DET THE)
                                                        (ADJ)
                                                        (MODIFIERS)))
                                              (OBJ (NP (N REPAIR)
                                                       (DET NIL)
```

```
                                              (ADJ
                                               EXTENSIVE
                                               ENGINE)
                                              (MODIFIERS)))
                                   (INDOBJ NIL)
                                   (PPS NIL))))))))
      (INDOBJ NIL)
      (PPS NIL)))
  (INDOBJ NIL)
  (PPS NIL))
```

>> I want you to show me the planes which have poor
   maintenance records.

```
(S (VERB WANT)
   (SUBJ (NP (N I) (DET NIL) (ADJ) (MODIFIERS)))
   (OBJ (S (VERB SHOW)
           (SUBJ (NP (N YOU) (DET NIL) (ADJ) (MODIFIERS)))
           (OBJ (NP (N PLANE)
                    (DET THE)
                    (ADJ)
                    (MODIFIERS (S (VERB HAVE)
                                  (SUBJ (NP (N PLANE)
                                            (DET THE)
                                            (ADJ)
                                            (MODIFIERS)))
                                  (OBJ (NP (N RECORD)
                                           (DET NIL)
                                           (ADJ POOR MAINTENANCE)
                                           (MODIFIERS)))
                                  (INDOBJ NIL)
                                  (PPS NIL)))))
           (INDOBJ (NP (N I) (DET NIL) (ADJ) (MODIFIERS)))
           (PPS NIL)))
   (INDOBJ NIL)
   (PPS NIL))
```

7.4 Examples of Tracing States

The following example shows a trace of the action of the ATN network in
parsing a sentence. This trace was generated by evaluating (TRACE-STA-
TES *). Again, the input string is preceded by ">>" and the final value

POPed by the network is displayed at the end. Values POPed by final states have been abbreviated.

>> Which aircraft have very poor maintenance records?

```
in state S:
pushing to state NP:
    in state NP:
    in state NP:DET
    in state NP:DET
    failing from state NP:DET
    in state NP:N
    jump to state NP:END
    in state NP:END
    pop from state NP: with value (NP (N PLANE) ... )
jump to state S:SUBJ
in state S:SUBJ
in state S:V
pushing to state NP:
    in state NP:
    jump to state NP:DET
    in state NP:DET
    in state NP:DET
    in state NP:DET
    in state NP:DET
    in state NP:DET
    failing from state NP:DET
    in state NP:DET
    failing from state NP:DET
    in state NP:N
    jump to state NP:END
    in state NP:END
    pop from state NP: with value (NP (N RECORD) ... )
jump to state S:OBJ
in state S:OBJ
jump to state S:END
in state S:END
pop from state TOPLEVEL with value (S (VERB HAVE) ... )
```

```
(S (VERB HAVE)
   (SUBJ (NP (N PLANE) (DET WHICH) (ADJ) (MODIFIERS)))
   (OBJ (NP (N RECORD)
            (DET NIL)
            (ADJ VERY POOR MAINTENANCE)
            (MODIFIERS)))
   (INDOBJ NIL)
   (PPS NIL))
```

7.5 Examples of Tracing Registers

This example shows a trace of the values assigned to ATN registers as
well. This was achieved by evaluating (TRACE-STATES *) and (TRACE-REG *).

```
>> I want you to list those planes

in state S:
pushing to state NP:
   in state NP:
   jump to state NP:DET
   in state NP:DET
   setting register ADJ to  (I)
   in state NP:DET
   failing from state NP:DET
   setting register N to  I
   in state NP:N
   jump to state NP:END
   in state NP:END
   pop from state NP: with value (NP (N I) ... )
setting register SUBJ to  (NP (N I) ... )
jump to state S:SUBJ
in state S:SUBJ
setting register V to WANT
in state S:V
pushing to state NP:
   in state NP:
   jump to state NP:DET
   in state NP:DET
   setting register ADJ to  (YOU)
   in state NP:DET
   failing from state NP:DET
   setting register N to  YOU
   in state NP:N
```

```
      jump to state NP:END
      in state NP:END
      pop from state NP: with value (NP (N YOU) ... )
  setting register OBJ to (NP (N YOU) ... )
  jump to state S:OBJ
  in state S:OBJ
  pushing to state NP:
      in state NP:
      jump to state NP:DET
      in state NP:DET
      failing from state NP:DET
      failing from state NP:
  sending register SUBJ to (NP (N YOU) ... )
  pushing to state S:SUBJ
      in state S:SUBJ
      setting register V to LIST
      in state S:V
      pushing to state NP:
          in state NP:
          setting register DET to  THOSE
          in state NP:DET
          setting register ADJ to  (PLANE)
          in state NP:DET
          failing from state NP:DET
          in state NP:DET
          failing from state NP:DET
          in state NP:DET
          failing from state NP:DET
          setting register N to  PLANE
          in state NP:N
          jump to state NP:END
          in state NP:END
          pop from state NP: with value (NP (N PLANE) ... )
      setting register OBJ to (NP (N PLANE) (DET THOSE) ... )
      jump to state S:OBJ
      in state S:OBJ
      jump to state S:END
      in state S:END
      pop from state S:SUBJ with value (S (VERB LIST) ... )
```

```
setting register OBJ to  (S (VERB LIST) ... )
jump to state S:END
in state S:END
pop from state TOPLEVEL with value (S (VERB WANT) ... )

(S (VERB WANT)
    (SUBJ (NP (N I) (DET NIL) (ADJ) (MODIFIERS)))
    (OBJ (S (VERB LIST)
            (SUBJ (NP (N YOU) (DET NIL) (ADJ) (MODIFIERS)))
            (OBJ (NP (N PLANE) (DET THOSE) (ADJ) (MODIFIERS)))
            (INDOBJ NIL)
            (PPS NIL)))
    (INDOBJ NIL)
    (PPS NIL))
```

8.0 REFERENCES

[Bate78]   Bates, M., "The Theory and Practice of Augmented Transition
            Network Grammars", in Natural Language Communication with
            Computers, Leonard Bolc (ed.), Springer Verlag, 1978.

[Bobr69]   Bobrow, D., "An Augmented State Transition Network Analysis
            Procedure", in Proceedings of the First International Joint
            Conference on Artificial Intelligence, 1969.

[Burt76a]   Burton, R. and Brown, J., "Multiple Representation of Know-
            ledge for World Reasoning" in 'Representation and Understan-
            ding', Bobrow and Collins (eds.), Academic Press, 1975.

[Burt76b]   Burton, R., "Semantic Grammar: An Engineering Technique for
            Constructing Natural Language Understanding Systems", BBN
            Report No. 3453, Bolt Beranek and Newman, 1976.

[Fini77a]   Finin, T.W., "An Interpreter and Compiler for Augmented Tran-
            sition Networks", Report T-48, Coordinated Science Laboratory,
            University of Illinois, 1977.

[Fini77b]   Finin, T.W. and Hadden, G., "Augmenting ATNs", Proceedings
            of the Fifth International Joint Conference on Artificial
            Intelligence, 1977.

[Fini78]   Finin, T.W., "Casting the RENDEZVOUS Analyzer Rules into
            Augmented Transition Network Form", IBM Research Report RJ
            2146(29409), IBM RESEARCH LAB., San Jose, CA, 1978.

[Gabr75]   Gabriel, R.P and Finin, T.W., "The LISP Editor", Working
            Paper 1, Advanced Automation Group, Coordinated Science Lab,
            University of Illinois, 1975

[Kay 75]   Kay, M., "Syntactic Processing and Functional Sentence Per-
            spective", Proceedings of the Conference on 'Theoretical
            Issues in Natural Language Processing', June 1975.

[Loza76]   Lozano-Perez, T., "Parsing Intensity Profiles", M.I.T. AI
            Memo 329, May 1975.

[Moon74]   Moon, D.A., "MacLISP Reference Manual", Project MAC, M.I.T.,
            1974.

[Simm73]   Simmons, R.F., "Semantic Networks: Their Computation and
            Use for Understanding English Sentences" in 'Computer Models
            of Thought and Language', R.C. Shank and K.M. Colby (Eds.),
            Freeman and Co, 1973

[Thor68]   Thorne, J.P., Bratley, P. and Dewar, H., "The Syntactic Ana-
            lysis of English by Machine" in Machine Intelligence 3,
            Donald Michie (ed.), 1968.

[Walt75]   Waltz, D.L., "Natural Language Access to a Large Data Base:
            an Engineering Approach", Advanced Papers of the Fourth In-
            ternational Joint Conference on Artificial Intelligence,1975.

[Walt76]   Waltz, D.L., et. al., "The PLANES System: Natural Language
            Access to a Large Data Base", Technical Report T-34, Coordi-
            nated Science Laboratory, University of Illinois, 1976.

[Walt78]   "An English Language QuestionAnswering System for a Large Re-
            lational Data Base", CACM vol. 21, July 1978.

[Wood70]   Woods, W.A., "Transition Network Grammars for Natural Langu-
            age Analysis", Communications of the ACM, October 1970.

[Wood72]   Woods, W.A., Kaplan, R.M., Nash-Webber, The Lunar Sciences
           Natural Language Information System: Final report, Bolt Bera-
           nek and Newman report No. 2378, June 1972.

An ATN Programming Environment

Thomas Christaller[1]

CONTENTS

---

[1] Research Unit for Information Science and Artificial Intelligence
University of Hamburg, Mittelweg 179, D-2000 HAMBURG 13

1.0   INTRODUCTION

The Augmented Transition Network Formalism [Woods 1970] is one of the
standard tools in natural language processing. In recent years some text
books about artificial intelligence present implementations of ATN interpreters and compilers [Winston 1978] [Charniak et. al. 1980]. Nevertheless these expositories can't present working systems.

The purpose here is to describe a running ATN system which is in use at
the linguistics department of the University of Bielefeld. The aim is
not to give all the idiosyncratics used in some specific tasks but a
well founded base. The implementation is done in a subset of MacLISP
[Moon 1976] on a telefunken computer TR440. Those features which may
not be available in other LISP dialects are mentioned in an appendix.

There exist excellent introduction texts to LISP and ATNs. It is assumed
that the reader is familiar with LISP as well as with ATNs. [Winston,
Horn, 1981] and [Bates 1978] should be consulted if any term or construct isn't defined in this paper. The arrangement of it is as follows.

The chapters 2 and 3 give a description of the language in which ATN
grammars can be written and some formal examples. Only main differences
to other ATN languages are described in greater detail.

In chapter 4 the implementation of an interpreter for the more basic
language constructs is given. While in chapter 5 the full interpreter
is described.

An incremental compiler is given in chapter 6. It compiles single states
of an ATN into LISP code. Therefore, it is easy to change a grammar
without recompiling it completely.

Because the representation of ATNs which is used here, is quite different to other implementations the whole chapter 7 is devoted to it. The
main difference is that a grammar and its parts are represented as items
in a data base. They are forward and backward connected with each another.

The chapters 8 and 9 describe the interfaces for a special debugging
component and the LISP editor. The first is realized by some modifications of the interpreter. The second one makes use of the special representation scheme for ATNs and the possibility to extend the LISP editor by user-defined commands.

This work wouldn't be possible if there were not a lot of people working with this environment or implemented parts of it. Especially I want to thank Tony Jameson, who implemented an earlier version of the interpreter and compiler. Manfred Gehrke, Heinz Backes, and Dieter Metzing, who pointed out to me a lot of bugs and discussed several aspects of the system with me. Tim Finin, who gave me the code of his ATN interpreter and compiler.

2.0   A SHORT DEFINITION OF THE ATN LANGUAGE

There are a lot of different ATN dialects. In this chapter you will find the definition of another one. It is based upon the definition in [Bates 1978]. Some short remarks are included to explain the differences. It is assumed that the reader is familiar at least with one ATN-dialect.

The definitions are given for a linearized form of ATNs using the following conventions. Terminal symbols are in capital letters while nonterminals are in lowercase and enclosed in angle brackets. The '*' is the Kleene operator and the parenthesises are the list delimiters in LISP. Optional parts are enclosed in curled brackets.

2.1   Arcs

This language distinguishes between two kinds of arcs. The first one are those which define the connections between states, i.e. they define which pathes exist through a grammar. The second kind are those called meta-arcs. They do not define any connections but change the parsing strategy to some extent.

In general the definition of an instance of each simple arc has the following form:

    (<arctype> <special test> <action> * <destination>)

whereas the definition of a meta arc looks like:

    (<metaarctype> <arc> *)

(WORD <words> <action> * <destination>)
    <words> is either a single word or a list of words. A WORD arc is
    tried when the actual word is equal to <words> or a member of it.

(JUMP <destination> <action> *)
   doesn't consume any word from the input.

(TST <label> <action> * <destination>)
   a TST arc is tried when the functional argument <label> applied to
   the actual word gives a non-NIL result.

(SEEK <phrasetype> <pre-action> * <action> * <destination>)
   is successful if there is an instance of <phrasetype> in the input
   beginning with the actual word. This arc type is normally called
   PUSH and <phrasetype> is the name of an initial state of a network.

(SEND (<phrasetype> *) <form> <action> *)
   is successful if the last SEEK arc encountered during the evaluation
   searches for an instance in the list of (<phrasetype> *). This arc
   type is normally called POP and doesn't check if it corresponds to
   the phrasetype of the last SEEK arc.

(ROOT <roots> <action> * <destination>)
   is successful if the normalform in the lexical entry of the actual
   word is equal to <roots> or a member of it.

(CAT <categories> <action> * <destination>)
   is an abbreviation for a bundle of arcs (described in more detail
   below). Is successful if the actual word has a lexical entry with a
   category which is equal to <categories> or a member of it.

(GROUP <arc> *)
   Non-determinism is switched off for the arcs which are arguments of
   a GROUP arc. If the arcset of each state in an ATN is enclosed in a
   GROUP arc, this ATN will be evaluated deterministically in the formal
   sense of this term.

(TRYPAR <arc> *)
   Every path starting with an arc enclosed in a TRYPAR arc is evaluated
   in parallel, i.e. it provides breadth-first search.

(TRYSEQ <arc> *)
   Every path starting with an arc enclosed in a TRYSEQ arc is evaluated
   in sequence, i.e. it provides depth-first search.

2.2 Actions and Forms

Because an ATN-Language should be independent of any grammar theory,
this particular language pre-defines only a small set of actions and
forms. It is possible to use any function defined in LISP as an action
or as a form. The grammar writer is responsible to prove which properties of the theory are reflected by a specific action or form. The difference between actions and forms is that an action serves only for producing some side effect while a form produces a value. The value of a
form can be used as argument of an action.

(SETR <register> <value> { <register> <value> ...})
   The assignment operator in a single network. The assignment of <value>
   to <register> is done in a sequential manner.

(SENDR <register> <value> { <level> })
   may be seen as a parameter passing device for a subcomputation.
   should only be used on a SEEK arc as pre-action.

(LIFTR <register> <value> { <level> })
   may be seen as a multiple value device from a subcomputation.
   should only be used on a SEND arc.

(VERIFY <test> { <label> })
   This action allows to include an arbitrary number of additional tests
   on an arc besides the special test on some arcs. It is possible to
   use any function defined in LISP as <test>. The only important thing
   is, that depending on the value of that function the actual arc is
   blocked, i.e. if fails, or following actions are processed. The optional <label> argument gives the user some control over the normal
   backtracking regime. It has the following options:

   SEEK   the actual subcomputation fails
   TOP-LEVEL   the whole parse fails
   <state>   the computation starting with the state <state> fails,
               i.e. an alternative is seeked from the state before
               <state>.

(GETR <register> { <level> })
   This is the only form for registers in this ATN-language. It retrieves
   the content of <register>. It distinguishes not between a register
   with content NIL and a register, which has no content, i.e. it is un-
   declared.

The next two forms realize a simple look ahead feature. They inspect the tokens to the right of the actual token, i.e. tokens which are not yet accepted. This is of great use to avoid unnecessary recursive calls of networks, e.g. a network analyzing a prepositional phrase should only be invoked if the next token is a preposition.

(LOODAHEADW <wordlist>)
    It returns T(rue) if the next word is a member of <wordlist> otherwise it returns NIL.

(LOOKAHEADC <categories>)
    It returns T(rue) if the lexical category of the next word is a member of <categories> otherwise it returns NIL.

Using these two forms, e.g. on a SEEK arc, it is necessary that they are evaluated before the invoked network takes over the control. Therefore, there must be the possibility to mark an action as a pre-action. This can be done with the '>'-prefix. The example of a subnet call for analyzing a prepositional phrase may look like

    (SEEK PP (>(VERIFY (LOOKAHEADC PREP))) (TO <somewhere>))

which means that the VERIFY action is executed as a pre-action. It will block the SEEK arc if the next token has not the lexical category PREP.

The non-terminal <destination> which occurs on several arcs represents the state in a network to which the transition function will go if such an arc was successful. With the exception of the JUMP arc this <destination> is written as an instance of the (pseudo-) action TO.

(TO <state>)
    moves immediately to <state>.

Besides the possibility to define his/her own actions and forms a grammar writer can define new arc types. To do that, it isn't necessary to change the interpreter at any point. In the chapter about the interpreter all arcs mentioned above are described in great detail. This may serve as a guide how to define new types.

Normally, you will find some kind of structure building functions in other ATN languages. Such functions suffer from the fact that they are related to a specific grammar theory or task for which an ATN is writ-

ten. Therefore, they should not be included in the general definition.
In any case one should not use the BUILDQ function described in [Woods
1970]. It is difficult to understand and inefficient. A good solution
is proposed in [Pereira, Warren 1980].

For the same reason the definitions of the CAT- and ROOT-arcs don't belong to the general definition of an ATN language. They are included
nevertheless because they are frequently used in ATNs independently of
the linguistic theory which the ATNs model. But keep in mind that their
correct operation depends on a specific definition of the lexical entry
data structure for the tokens.

2.3 Phrasetypes

A phrasetype is a data structure which connects the name of a phrasetype with a state in an ATN. This makes it possible to refer on a SEEK
or SEND arc to a linguistic category instead of a procedural entity,
i.e. a state.

Besides a more theoretical perspicuity the use of phrasetypes allows a
greater conceptual factorization of a grammar. One state may serve as
an initial state for more than one phrasetype. So one network can reflect the similarities between different phrasetypes. The differences
then can be represented by SEND arcs leaving the network, which differs
from each another in the following sense. Each SEND arc is responsible
for some phrasetypes. So either the end state for different phrasetypes
may be different or the result. For a more detailed discussion see
[Woods 1980].

2.4 States, Networks, and Machines

Besides arcs the states are the second main data structure in an ATN.
Normally, they are defined as

    <arcset> ::= (<state> <arc> *)

where <state> is the name of the state and <arc> denotes a leaving arc
written in the syntactic form described earlier. In practice that means
there is a function say ARCSET with two arguments. One is the name for
a state and the second a list of leaving arcs. The result of a call of
this function will create a data structure where the state name serves
as a pointer to the list of arcs.

In a very straightforward implementation that is sufficient. But if the grammar writer wishes to be supported by a programming environment this is not enough. The reason is that every state is treated as a singular entity which is unrelated to any other state in a grammar. There is only an indirect connection from a state to each destination in a leaving arc.

Therefore, a state here is a more complex data structure. It may be described as

    <arcset> ::= (<inarcs> <state> <outarcs>)

i.e. a state name serves as a pointer to the outarcs set as well as to the inarcs set of a state in an ATN.

Besides this backward and forward connection of states every state is explicitly related to one network. Some states in a network are marked as initial states. This is done when a phrasetype is defined. An initial state is too connected with the phrasetypes for which it serves as an initial state.

A network and a machine, i.e. a grammar, are data structures too, whose instances are given a name. A network is linked to the set of states which belong to it. In addition a network 'knows' to which machine it belongs. On the other hand a machine name is associated with the list of its networks and the phrasetype whose instances it can analyze.

Arcs, states, networks, and one machine are therefore organized in a hierarchy. From every point it is possible to reach any other point in the hierarchy. Phrasetypes are linked to states and sometimes to machines. Therefore, a complete ATN grammar is a complex network similar to semantic networks [Quillian 1968] . The advantage of this approach is the ease of defining a powerful editor for ATNs.

2.5 Miscellaneous

As in other ATN languages this one has too some predefined variables which are quite useful. There are two variables which are pointers into the input string. One is called '*' and holds normally the actual word. The other is '**" and holds the root or normalform of the actual word.

The '*' is used for a different purpose on a SEEK arc. Normally it does not make any sense to refer to an actual word when the requested phrasetype was analyzed. On the other hand the remaining (post-) actions on a

SEEK arc may use the result of the subanalysis. This result, i.e. the value of the form argument of the SEND arc leaving this subanalysis, is stored in '*'. Any occurence of '*' in the postactions on a SEEK arc is a reference to this result.

Another variable is a counter for the depth of recursion. Its name is ATN-CL. It is initialized with 1, increased by 1 every time a SEEK arc is evaluated, and decreased by 1 respectively on a SEND arc. This may be used to access registers higher up or lower down than the actual level.

Besides the definition of a grammar you must supply a lexicon as well. The arcs WORD, ROOT, and CAT rely on the definition of this lexicon. In this presentation it is expected to be a full form lexicon. Each entry must be associated with the appropriate word. Its syntax is

   (<category> NF <root> <feature> <value> <feature> <value> ...)

where <category> is a linguistic category used by CAT arcs. NF is the predefined feature for the normalform and its value is the root of the given word.

(GETF <feature>)

   extracts the value of <feature> from the lexical entry of the actual word.

(GETLEXENTRY <word>)

   gets the list of lexical entries of a given word. It it has none, it requests at least one from the user interactively.

3.0 EXAMPLES of ATNs

The following chapter gives ATN grammars for some formal languages. They will serve as demonstration objects in the next chapters. Most of the constructs defined in the last chapter are used. In so far these ATNs are also useful to test the implementation of various parts of the system.

An example of one of the simplest formal grammar is

G1:   S ---> ab
       S ---> abS

which defines the language (ab)^n with n>0. A graphical representation of an ATN grammar is given in the following figure.

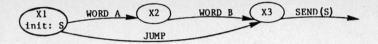

Figure 3.1: State Diagram for G1

The linear representation in figure 3.2 doesn't reflect that X1 is the initial state and how states are connected with their leaving arcs. This is explained in chapter 7. On the other hand the SEND arc at state X3 has two additional arguments. The T is the form argument, i.e. the result of a successful analysis, and the VERIFY action ensures that this arc is only used when the end of string is detected.

X1:   (WORD A (TO X2))

X2:   (WORD B (TO X3))

X3:   (SEND (S) T (VERIFY (END-OF-STRING?)))
        (JUMP X1)

Figure 3.2: Linear Representation of G1

The next example is a context free grammar

G2:   S ---> ab
        S ---> aSb

which defines the language a^n b^n with n>0. The following type of diagram is sometimes called a Recursive Transition Network (RTN). In general it may consist of a set of mutually recursive diagrams.

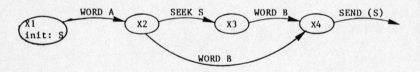

Figure 3.3: An RTN for the Grammar G2

Its linear representation is very similar to G1 so it may be omitted here. The following example looks quite complicated written in form of rewrite rules:

```
G3:    S ---> aSC
       S ---> aB
      BC ---> bBc
      cC ---> Cc
       B ---> bc
```

which defines the language a^n b^n c^n with n>0. But in the ATN formalism we can start with a grammar similar to the RTN above. This grammar realizes a context free one for the language a^n b^n c^m with n,m>0 and in general n=m. But with registers and the VERIFY action we can keep track of the number of the letters a,b, and c and ensure that they are equal.

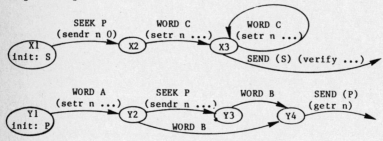

Fig. 3.4: An ATN for the Grammar G3

The linear form of this grammar is as follows:

X1:   (SEEK P (SENDR N O) (SETR N *) (TO X2))

X2:   (WORD C (SETR N (1- (GETR N)) (TO X3))

X3:   (WORD C (SETR N (1- (GETR N)) (TO X3))
      (SEND (S) (VERIFY (ZEROP (GETR N)))))

Y1:   (WORD A (SETR N (1+ (GETR N))) (TO Y2))

Y2:   (WORD B (TO Y4))
      (SEEK P (SENDR N (GETR N)) (TO Y3))

Y3:   (WORD B (TO Y4))

Y4:   (SEND (P) (GETR N))

Figure 3.5: The Linear Representation for the ATN of G3

The grammars G1 to G3 are unambiguous. Therefore, at every state where more than one arc is leaving it, these arcs may be grouped together in a GROUP arc. This will force the interpreter to evaluate these grammars deterministically. Care must be taken when grouping a SEEK arc. Additional look ahead has to be done there. Otherwise a subnetwork is tried when it shouldn't.

4.0   THE BASIC INTERPRETER

The heart of the system is the interpreter. Its purpose is to give the user flexibility in choosing the appropriate parsing strategy, modifying the existing ATN-language, and interfacing to all the other modules in the environment. This is achieved by a careful design and modularization of the interpretation process. There is no monolithic interpreter but a set of specialists.

4.1 Design

The evaluation of an ATN is divided into sub-evaluations along the syntax definition of the ATN-language: evaluation of a state, an arc, and actions. To implement the standard parsing strategy, i.e. top-down, depth-first with backtracking, it is possible to rely completely on recursion [Finin 1978]. If the grammar writer wants to replace this default strategy by another one he may use one of the so-called meta-arcs. Last but not least there is a monitor which creates the necessary binding environment.

Because the monitor is on top of the interpretation process we can start with it anyway. It does three things. First, it initializes all of the local and global variables. The most important are POP-STACK which provides recursion in ATNs, several pointers into the input, and REG-STACK to keep track of register bindings in the networks. The second thing is, to hand over the control to the state evaluation specialist with the initial state of a given ATN.

As mentioned above the evaluation is done in a recursive manner, i.e. if the first state finds a successful arc, it will give the control to the destination state of that arc. This will be evaluated by the transition specialist recursively until eventually control is coming back to the monitor. The result is either success or failure. Reporting that result is the third task of the monitor.

The three tasks of the monitor:

1. Initialize the following data structures and variables
   REG-STACK
   POP-STACK
   SYNTAX
   CSYNTAX
   *
   **

2. Hand over control to the state evaluation specialist with the default parsing strategy.

3. Print the result of the analysis and save it.

Figure 4.1: Monitor of the ATN-interpreter

Evaluation of a state means to define the transition function for an automata equivalent to the given ATN. This system allows to change the parsing strategy dynamically. Therefore, the transition function is a local function. How this is achieved is explained in later sections. At the moment it is assumed that this function realizes the 'classical' ATN evaluation strategy. It's name is TO1.

The transition function takes two arguments. The first is the name of the next state in the ATN and the second is a flag which reports if the pointer into the input should be moved or not. Therefore, this flag is called NOMOVEFLAG. If it is NIL the pointer should move otherwise it should not.

The function TO1 decides in which environment the given state is to be evaluated. This depends only on the value of NOMOVEFLAG. After choosing an environment it gives control to the state evaluating specialist which is called EVAL-STATE.

EVAL-STATE discriminates three cases. Either the given state is a compiled one (see section about the ATN-Compiler). In this case it gives control immediately to the state itself, or the given state has an arc-set of cardinality one. In this case EVAL-STATE ensures that the backtracking can skip this state because it has no alternative. If there are two or more arcs leaving the state, the untried alternatives must be saved. In both of the last cases control is given to the general arc specialist.

This specialist is named EVAL-ARC. It is called for each arc independently of the type. Its purpose is to isolate possible side effects when
evaluating a specific arc. But the only side effects an arc may have are
modifications of the content of some registers. Therefore, the REG-STACK
variable is isolated by creating a new binding environment for it. Every
arc type is implemented by a LISP-function with the name as the arc type.
So the only thing EVAL-ARC has to do is to evaluate a given arc using
the EVAL function of LISP.

4.2 Arc Specialists

The next sections are a little bit more complicated because they describe in some detail every individual arc specialist. They all have in
common that they are defined as macros [Charniak et.al. 80]. The reason
is, that the expansion of such a macro call will give the most efficient
LISP-code for the given arc. The ATN-compiler relies on that fact. With
this technique it isn't necessary to provide the compiler with detailed
knowledge about the function of an arc. A drawback of this is that the
interpretation is significantly slower (by a factor of 5 compared to
LISP-compiled ATNs). Every arc specialist instead assumes that all actions are defined LISP-functions.

The result of the expansion for an arc which leaves control in a given
network is the following:

```
(AND ,<special test>
     (PROGN ,@<actions>
            (TO1 ,<destination> ,<nomoveflag>)))
```

Figure 4.2: Expansion Scheme of Simple Arcs

The notion used in this figure is a blend of the backquote (see appendix A and [LISPMACHINE]) and Backus-Naur form. Every string in capital
letters is a terminal one. Every string in lowercase letters enclosed
in angle brackets refers to a variable or function call which is computed when evaluating an arc. If such a string is preceded by a comma,
then the value of this variable is taken. When a comma atsign prefix
occurs, the value must be a list and is spliced into the surrounding
list.

The scheme should be read as: the code of an arc is a boolean AND. The
first argument of it is the special test of the arc if there is any.

The second argument is a sequence consisting of all of the actual actions of an arc and the last call in this sequence is that of the transition function with the destination of an arc and the appropriate value
for NOMOVEFLAG.

The effect of this arrangement is that only when the <special test> evaluates to non-NIL the sequence of actions will be evaluated. The only
action which is allowed to block an arc is the VERIFY action. It has
some mechanism to give the control back to the EVAL-STATE specialist.
If the control is given back either because the <special test> fails or
a VERIFY action blocks the arc, the EVAL-STATE function looks if there
is any alternative at the actual state. If there is one it will give
control to the next arc otherwise it returns NIL.

This simple scheme can only be used for the JUMP, ROOT, TEST, and WORD
arc types. For every other type a more or less complicated scheme holds.
In the following figures the exact schemes for the above mentioned simple
arc types are given.

```
'(PROGN (SETQ ** (GETF NF))
        ,@<actions>
        (TO1 ,<destination> T))
```

Figure 4.3: Expansion for the JUMP arc

which means, set the variable ** to the normalform of the actual word.
Then evaluate the sequence of actions if there are any. If no VERIFY
action blocks the arc, then call the transition function with the destination of the JUMP-arc and NOMOVEFLAG=T(rue).

```
'(AND (MEMQ (SETQ ** (GETF NF))
            ,<list of root forms>)
      (PROGN ,@<actions>
             (TO1 ,<destination> NIL)))
```

Figure 4.4: Expansion for the ROOT arc

If the normal form of the actual word is a member of the given list of
root forms, then evaluate the sequence of actions and call the transition function in the same manner as for the JUMP arc type.

```
'(AND (MEMQ *
            ,<list of words>)
      (PROGN (SETQ ** (GETF NF))
            ,@<actions>
            (TO1 ,<destination> NIL)))
```

Figure 4.5: Expansion for the WORD arc

If the actual word is a member of the given list of words, then proceed
as in the case of a JUMP arc.

```
'(AND (,<label> *)
      (PROGN (SETQ ** (GETF NF))
            ,@<actions>
            (TO1 ,<destination> NIL)))
```

Figure 4.6: Scheme for the TEST arc

The function with name label is called with the actual word as argument. If the value of this function call is non-NIL, it proceeds as in
the case of a WORD arc.

An example may demonstrate this mechanism. Assume the following arc is
given:

```
(WORD B (SETR N (1- (GETR N))) (TO S4-B))
```

This will expand to:

```
(AND (MEMQ * '(B))
     (PROGN (SETR N (1- (GETR N)))
            (TO1 'S4-B NIL)))
```

More complicated are the schemes for those arc types which provide recursion in the ATN-language. These arcs are called SEEK and SEND. Both
are using auxiliary functions which create a new binding environment
for the variables ATN-CL, REG-STACK, and POP-STACK.

Every state on a path through an ATN is evaluated recursively using the
internal stack of the LISP system. Therefore, it isn't possible to implement recursion in an ATN with the same stack. (See [Charniak, et.al.
1980] for an implementation using the LISP stack for recursion in ATNs.)

The ATN interpreter uses an explicit stack which is called POP-STACK.
Every entry in it consists of a suspended computation of a SEEK arc
and a phrasetype. Such an entry is pushed on it when a SEEK arc is evaluated. A SEND arc will pop the last entry from POP-STACK. This stack
is initialized with the entry

    (<phrasetype of a given ATN-grammar> T)

The suspended computation consists of those actions on a SEEK arc which
are not explicitly marked or known as a preaction. Remember that (TO
<state>) is treated as an action and should be the last one in a list
of actions. The phrasetype in a POP-STACK entry ensures that always a
corresponding SEND arc is used to resume the interpretation of a SEEK
arc.

```
'(PROGN ,@<pre-actions>
        (LET (ATN-CL (1+ ,<atn-cl>)
              POP-STACK (CONS (MAKE-ENTRY ',<actions>
                                          ',<phrasetype>)
                              POP-STACK))
            (TO1 (INIT-STATE ',<phrasetype>)
                 T)))
```

Figure 4.7: Expansion for the SEEK arc

which means: evaluate the sequence of <pre-actions>. Create then a new
environment in which the transition function is called with the initial
state of a network which parses an instance of the required phrasetype.
If in an actual parse a successful path is found at its end a SEND arc
will be evaluated. It will resume the computation of the SEEK arc with
the saved actions on POP-STACK.

```
'(AND [MEMQ ',(PHRASETYPE:POP-STACK-ENTRY
                (TOP-OF POP-STACK))
            ',<phrasetypes>]
      [PROGN ,@<actions>
             (LET (* ,<form>
                   REG-STACK (CLEAR-REGS ATN-CL REG-STACK)
                   ATN-CL (1- ,<atn-cl>)
                   POP-STACK (CDR POP-STACK))
                 (COND
                   [(TERMINATED?)
                    (TERMINATE-PARSE *)])
```

```
, @(ACTIONS:POP-STACK-ENTRY
    (TOP-OF POP-STACK)) ] )
```

Figure 4.8: Expansion for the SEND arc

After checking that the saved phrasetype on POP-STACK is compatible with those given on a SEND arc the actions on the SEND arc are evaluated. This is done in the binding environment of the subcomputation. Then a new binding environment is created which in some sense restores that binding which existed at the time of the corresponding SEEK arc.

Two variables must be rebound in addition of those bounded by the SEEK arc. This is the variable * which normally is a pointer into the input string. But this will hold the result of the SEND arc, i.e. the value of the form argument. The other one is REG-STACK. The function CLEAR-REGS ensures that all registers which were set in the actual network are cleared, i.e. they are not accessible any longer.

The next thing which is done is to check if the parse is finished. If so it gives immediately the control back to the monitor with the result of this parse. Otherwise it continues the parsing. The termination condition is very simple. The SEND arc must be evaluated on the top level of recursion, i.e. the value of the variable POP-STACK must be NIL.

The most complicated scheme is that for the CAT-arc. The reason is that a single CAT arc stands for a bundle of arcs. But the cardinality of it depends on the number of lexical entries for the actual word under consideration. Therefore, a CAT arc must iterate through the list of lexical entries while supporting the default parsing strategy.

```
'(FOR [ENTRY IN (LEXICAL-ENTRIES *)]
    [DO
        (CATCH
            (AND [MEMQ (CATEGORY ENTRY)
                    ,<list of categories>)
                [PROGN ,@<actions>
                    (TO1 ,<destination> NIL)])
            EVAL-ARC)])
```

Figure 4.9: Expansion for the CAT arc

If every word has only one lexical entry this scheme may be replaced by
the inner AND. The call of this AND is quite similar to the ROOT, WORD,
and TEST arc. It says if the lexical category of the actual word is a
member of the given list of categories then evaluate the sequence of actions and call the transition function with the destination of the CAT
arc and NOMOVEFLAG=NIL.

The code (CATCH ... EVAL-ARC) is only necessary to prohibit any VERIFY
action on the CAT arc to give the control back to the state specialist.
How this function is explained in the chapter of actions. The FOR loop
ensures that every lexical entry is tried before a CAT arc fails. (For
CATCH and THROW see appendix A.)

The VERIFY action will execute a (THROW NIL EVAL-ARC) if its argument
evaluates to NIL. In case of the CAT arc this is CATCHed inside the FOR.
If there is any lexical entry left, it is used instead. Otherwise the
CAT arc fails.

4.3 Evaluation Specialists

The generalization of the technique used for the CAT arc is used to implement the backtracking algorithm for the ATN interpreter. At every
choice point is a function which iterates through all alternatives. If
an alternative is successfully evaluated control will never come back
to this point. The control will only come back if backtracking occurs.
Either explicitly using a THROW or implicitly using the normal function
call and return mechanism in LISP. Anyway, the evaluation of each choice
is encapsulated in a CATCH with label EVAL-ARC.

As it is mentioned above the state specialist is responsible for that.
A simple version of it is shown in the next figure.

```
(DE EVAL-STATE (STATE)
   (FOR  [ARC IN (GETOUTARCS STATE)]
        [DO (CATCH (EVAL-ARC ARC)
                   EVAL-ARC)]))
```

Figure 4.10: The State Specialist EVAL-STATE. First Version

The evaluation of every arc is done by EVAL-ARC.

```
(DE EVAL-ARC (ARC)
   (LET (REG-STACK REG-STACK)
```

```
              (EVAL ARC)))
```

   Figure 4.11: The Arc Specialist EVAL-ARC. First Version

What is left is the transition function TO1.

```
   (DE TO1 (STATE NOMOVEFLAG)
     (COND
        [NOMOVEFLAG (EVAL-STATE STATE)]
        [T (LET (SYNTAX (REST SYNTAX)
                 CSYNTAX <actual word with lexical entries>
                 * <actual word>
                 ** <get normalform from the first lexical entry>)
             (EVAL-STATE STATE))]))
```

   Figure 4.12: The Transition Function TO1. First Version

On several arc types the destination of the arc is given by the action
TO. It is defined as a macro which expands to a call of the transition
function with the appropriate arguments.

```
   (DEFMACRO TO (STATE)
     '(TO1 ',STATE ,(NON-CONSUMING-ARC? ARC)))
```

   Figure 4.13: The TO-action. First Version

The variable ARC is here a free variable. But TO is always evaluated in
the scope of EVAL-ARC so it refers to the actual arc. The predicate NON-
COSUMING-ARC? gives T(rue) if the actual arc is a non-cosuming one otherwise NIL.

The whole evaluation of an ATN may be seen as nested circles. Each circ-
le is either created by a FOR to ensure backtracking. The second possibility is a CATCH which ensures that a VERIFY action aborts only that
computation specified by its second argument. Or it is created by a new
LAMBDA-environment to isolate side effects of every arc.

To complete this first run through the evaluation specialists the code
of the monitor is given.

```
(DE PARSE1 (STATE SYNTAX)
  (LET (POP-STACK (LIST (MAKE-POP-STACK-ENTRY
                          (PHRASETYPE:STATE STATE)
                          (LIST T)))
        CSYNTAX (CURR-SYNTAX SYNTAX)
        * (CURR-WORD SYNTAX))
       ** NIL
       ATN-CL 1
       REG-STACK NIL)
    (CATCH (CATCH (TO1 STATE T)
                  EVAL-ARC)
           TOP-LEVEL)))
```

Figure 4.14: The Monitor PARSE1. First Version

The monitor assumes that the input string is given in advance. In the
next chapter we will see a version were this is not necessary. The variables CSYNTAX, *, and ** are pointers into the input. The value of
CSYNTAX holds the actual word together with its lexical definition. *
holds the actual word and ** holds the root form of the actual word. Only on a SEND arc the * is set to the form argument of the SEND arc.

The variables REG-STACK and ATN-CL are discussed below. The POP-STACK
variable is initialized as mentioned above. The first entry is the trivial sequence of actions (T) and the phrasetype which is associated with
the initial state of a grammar.

4.4 Register Operations

Normally an ATN doesn't only accept or reject an input string but it
gives the analysis of that string according to the grammar theory. To
achieve this, a grammar writer has to store information gathered during
the analysis. For this purpose are the registers.

A register is similar to variables in normal programming languages. The
difference is that they don't need any declaration in before hand. The
first time a register is used it is declared. One consequence is that
there is no difference between an empty register and an unused one.

The bindings of registers are stored in an association list using a deep
binding strategy, i.e. the latest bound register is retrieved faster than
earlier bindings. It is not sufficient to build an entry in this association list of the register name and its value.

The reason is again that registers are not declared. Especially, the registers used in one network are not the formal parameters of that network. On the other hand a network may be called recursively. Therefore, to retrieve the value of a register one has to refer to its name and the recursion level.

The actual recursion level is given by a variable ATN-CL. Its value is an integer and it is initialized with 1. An entry in the association list has the form

    ((<register> . <level>) . <value>)

to retrieve a value one has to specify the name of the register and the level on which the register should be looked up.

All register operations are based on two primitives **GETR** for retrieving and **SETR** for assigning values. Both use the variable REG-STACK as the actual association list. Here are the definitions:

```
(DE  **SETR** (REGISTER LEVEL VALUE)
     (PUSH REG-STACK
           (CONS (CONS REGISTER LEVEL)
                 VALUE)))
(DE  **GETR** (REGISTER LEVEL)
(CDR (ASSOC (CONS REGISTER LEVEL)
            REG-STACK)))
```

    Figure 4.15: The Basic Register Operations

It is obvious from the code that to reset a register means to add a new entry at the front of REG-STACK. This is necessary because backtracking may occur and requires to reinstall the old register bindings. Therefore, a direct updating of a register can result in a wrong register environment. Instead of maintaining seperate association lists for every choice point this technique merges common parts of these lists together [Woods 1978].

All the other register operations are defined as macros which expand to calls of these functions. The most important are SETR and GETR. They differ only from **SETR** and **GETR** respectively that it isn't necessary to specify the level and to quote the register name. Both assume that the given register should be set or its value retrieved on the current level of recursion.

```
(DEFMACRO SETR (REGISTER VALUE)
    '(**SETR** ',REGISTER ATN-CL , VALUE))

(DEFMACRO GETR (REGISTER)
    '(**GETR** ',REGISTER ATN-CL))
```

Figure 4.16: Register Operations in a Network

Sometimes it is very convenient to accumulate information in a register, i.e. to use it as a stack. There are two operations to increase the value ADDL and ADDR depending if you want to add to the left or right of the existing value. Similar there are two operations which decrease the value SUBL and SUBR.

```
(DEFMACRO ADDL (REGISTER VALUE)
    '(**SETR** ,REGISTER ATN-CL (CONS , VALUE
                                    (**GETR** ,REGISTER
                                         ATN-CL))))

(DEFMACRO ADDR (REGISTER VALUE)
    '(**SETR** ,REGISTER ATN-CL
              (APPEND (**GETR** ,REGISTER ATN-CL)
                     ,VALUE)))
```

Figure 4.17: Using Registers as Stacks

As mentioned above registers are not declared as formal parameters of a network. Nevertheless it is possible to pass registers from one level of recursion to another one. Two functions SENDR and LIFTR realize this. The function SENDR sends registers to a lower level while LIFTR lifts them to a higher level. Both take an optional argument to specify the level. If it is missing, they take the next higher or next lower level respectively.

```
(DEFMACRO SENDR (REGISTER VALUE LEVEL)
    '(**SETR** ,REGISTER
              ,(OR LEVEL
                   '(1+ ATN-CL))
              ,VALUE))
```

```
(DEFMACRO LIFTR (REGISTER VALUE LEVEL)
    '(**SETR** ,REGISTER
              ,(OR LEVEL
                   '(1- ATN-CL))
              ,VALUE))
```

Figure 4.18: Passing Registers

This implementation of register operations should be sufficient for simple applications. A grammar writer is hereby recommended to write his/
her own information saving and retrieving functions using the above ones.
One should bear in mind that every operation using **SETR** is an action
and those using **GETR are forms.

4.5 Examples of the Interpretation

In what follows are two traces using the trace of the LISP system are
shown. They should demonstrate the basic interpretation process. The
simple grammar G1 in chapter 3 is used. The monitor PARSE1 is called
with the initial state of that grammar and with a preprocessed form of
the string.

These tracings should be read as follows. Every function call is reported by giving the string '--->' followed by the function name and the
actual arguments of the function call. Every result of a function is
started with '<---' followed by the function name and the value. The
numbers before the arrows refer to the depth of recursion for this function.

The first example shows the analysis of the string "a b".

```
1 ---> parse1 : s1- ((a) (b))
  1 ---> to1 : s1- t
    1 ---> eval-state : s1-
      1 ---> eval-arc : (word a (to s1-a))
        1 ---> word : a ((to s1-a))
          1 ---> to : s1-a
            2 ---> to1 : s1-a nil
              2 ---> eval-state : s1-a
                2 ---> eval-arc : (word b (to s1-b))
                  2 ---> word : b ((to s1-b))
                    2 ---> to : s1-b
```

```
        3 ---> to1 : s1-b nil
      3 ---> eval-state : s1-b
    3 ---> eval-arc : (send t
              (verify (end-of-string?))
      1 ---> send : t ((verify
                    (end-of-string?)))
1 <--- parse1 : t
```

Figure 4.19: A Trace of the Interpretation Process

The monitor is called with the initial state of an ATN and with a list
of tokens. Each token itself is a list. The first element is the word
in the original input string and the others are the lexical entries for
it.

As this trace shows the control is handed from one specialist to another. In case of a successful parse the SEND arc returns control and the
result (in this case simply T) to the monitor. If the inputstring would
be "a b a b" the SEND arc will be blocked by the VERIFY action. The next
figure shows a trace beginning in this situation.

```
...
  3 ---> eval-state : s1-b
    3 ---> eval-arc : (send t (verify (end-of-string?)))
      1 ---> send : t ((verify (end-of-string?)))
      1 <--- send : nil
    3 <--- eval-arc : nil
    3 ---> eval-arc : (jump s1-a)
      1 ---> jump : s1- nil
        4 ---> to1 : s1-a t
          4 ---> eval-state : s1-
            4 ---> eval-arc : (word a (to s1-a))
              3 ---> word : (a) ((to s1-a))
                4 ---> to : s1-a
                  5 ---> to1 : s1-a nil
                    5 ---> eval-state : s1-a
                      5 ---> eval-arc : (word b (to s1-b))
                        4 ---> word : (b) ((to s1-b))
                          5 ---> to : s1-b
                            6 ---> to1 : s1-b nil
                              6 ---> eval-state : s1-b
...
```

Figure 4.20: A Trace of the Evaluation Process

If this interpreter is used to parse the string "a b a b a c" with the
same grammar as above backtracking will occur. This will force the state
specialist to look if there is any alternative left. But in the states
S1- and S1-A there was only one leaving arc. It should be possible to
bypass such states. The next version of EVAL-STATE allows this possibility.

```
(DE EVAL-STATE (STATE)
  (COND
      [(ONEP (LENGTH (GETOUTARCS STATE)))
       (EVAL-ARC (CAR (GETOUTARCS STATE)))]
      [T (FOR [ARC IN (GETOUTARCS STATE)]
              [DO (CATCH (EVAL-ARC ARC)
                         EVAL-ARC))]] ) ] ) )
```

Figure 4.21: The State Specialist EVAL-STATE. Second Version

I.e. if there is only one leaving arc one may omit the CATCH and the
iteration through the outarc set. When a single arc fails via backtracking the control will come back to EVAL-arc and therefore to EVAL-
STATE. But when this arc is blocked by a VERIFY action the control will
go back to the last CATCH with label EVAL-ARC. Such a CATCH might be
farer up in the function call hierarchy than the last EVAL-STATE.

5.0 THE ADVANCED INTERPRETER

In this chapter the interpreter is described which evaluates ATNs according to the language definition in chapter 2. This is achieved by slight
changes to the interpreter in the former chapter. The first modification
defines the transition function as a local function. This is necessary
if the grammar writer wants to use different parsing strategies.

Some examples of different strategies are presented as meta arcs. The
most important of them is the GROUP arc which allows local determinism.
The second modification ensures that the interpreter requests only new
input if it has processed the old one. After that a kind of looking a-
head is described. In recent natural language research it is stressed
that a parser has to be as deterministic as possible. It doesn't matter
if a parser is written for a natural language interface or a psycholo-
gical model of language comprehension. Looking ahead and the GROUP arc
are tools to achieve this goal.

5.1 The Local Transition Function

In the first version of the transition function TO1 the top-down depth-first strategy is realized. The next version stores as many definitions of the transition function as necessary on the property list of TO1. At any point of the interpretation one of these definitions may be active.

The monitor PARSE1 is changed to create a LAMBDA environment with the variable TO1 and binds it to the standard strategy. In this environment the interpretation of a given ATN is started.

```
(DE PARSE1 (STATE SYNTAX)
   (LET (POP-STACK (LIST (CONS (LIST T) PHRASETYPE))
         CSYNTAX (FIRST SYNTAX)
         * (FIRST (FIRST SYNTAX))
         ** NIL
         ATN-CL 1
         REG-STACK NIL)
      (LABEL (TO1 (GET 'TO1 'TOP-DOWN/DEPTH-FIRST))
         (CATCH (CATCH (TO1 STATE T)
                       EVAL-ARC)
                TOP-LEVEL))))
```

Figure 5.1: The Monitor. Second Version

To change the parsing strategy means here to change the binding of the variable TO1. (Remark: in some LISP implementations you are not allowed to use a variable in place of a function name. For an alternative see appendix A.) The value of (GET 'TO1 'TOP-DOWN/DEPTH-FIRST) is just the old function definition of TO1.

5.2 Meta Arcs

The meta arcs make use of the local definition of TO1. The first meta arc described is the GROUP arc. It takes an arbitrary number of arcs as arguments. The first successful arc is used definitely to find a parse, i.e. all remaining (untried) arcs will not be evaluated if the path eminating with this arc fails later on.

Like the EVAL-STATE specialist a GROUP arc must iterate through the given arcs. If an arc is blocked either by an unsatisfied special test or a VERIFY action the next arc should be evaluated. But if an arc is successfully evaluated this process should stop.

Therefore, a new transition definition is given. It is essentially the same as in the non-deterministic strategy. The difference is only in the specification of what should be done if the given state fails. In the normal strategy TO1 returns simply NIL. The returning itself is enough to force EVAL-STATE to evaluate the next arc. If there is none, it returns to the next higher EVAL-STATE etc.

But in a GROUP arc we know that in such a case the GROUP arc itself should fail no matter how many alternatives are left. This is done by THROWing out of the TO1 deterministic version to a CATCH in the GROUP arc. Because the scope of a GROUP arc is restricted to arcs this definition of TO1 should be changed to the old one if the first state on the choosen path out of a GROUP is passed, i.e. the deterministic TO1 has to create a new binding for TO1 with the old strategy.

```
(DF GROUP (ARCS)
   (CATCH (FOR [ARC IN ARCS]
              [DO (LET (TO1 (GET 'TO1 'DETERMINISTIC)
                       OLD-TO1 TO1)
                  (CATCH (EVAL-ARC ARC)
                         EVAL-ARC)] ) GROUP))
```

Figure 5.2: The GROUP arc. First Version

```
(DEPROP TO1
        (LAMBDA (STATE NOMOVEFLAG)
          (LETL (TO1 OLD-TO1)
            (COND
               [NOMOVEFLAG (SETQ * (CAR CSYNTAX))
                           (EVAL-STATE STATE)]
               [T (LETL (SYNTAX (REST SYNTAX)
                        CSYNTAX (FIRST (REST SYNTAX))
                        * (FIRST (FIRST (REST SYNTAX)))
                        ** NIL)
                  (EVAL-STATE STATE))])
            (THROW NIL GROUP)))
        DETERMINISTIC)
```

Figure 5.3: The Deterministic Transition Function

A simpler example is the meta arc TRYSEQ. Its purpose is to reinstall the top-down/depth-first strategy. The scope of this arc is not restric-

ted to the arcs which are the arguments of TRYSEQ but to all pathes
emerging from it. There is no need to define a new transition function.

```
(DF TRYSEQ (ARCS)
   (LABEL (TO (GET 'TO1 'TOP-DOWN/DEPTH-FIRST))
      (FOR (ARC IN ARCS)
            (DO (CATCH (EVAL-ARC ARC)
                        EVAL-ARC)))))
```

Figure 5.4: The TRYSEQ arc

The definitions of GROUP and TRYSEQ differs from the other definitions
given earlier. First they are not defined as macros, i.e. they do not
expand into 'optimal' code and the compiler have to treat them differently. Second they have no special test or whatsoever.

5.3 Read as you Need it

In all of the ATN systems published so far the interpreter assumes that
the input is given in advance, i.e. a parse can only start when the input is completed by a user. This is inconvenient either in a natural
language interface or in a comprehension model. Parsing should start
with the first token. A natural language interface has then at least
the possibility to take the initiative before an input is completed.
This may help to avoid unnecessary preprocessing and lexicon lookups.
In a comprehension model it is more obvious how much processing is done
while parsing a word.

These observations lead to an implementation which is useful too in a
multi stage processing system as in cascaded ATNs [Woods 1980]. The main
idea is to provide an ATN with an inputbuffer. Every time a input consuming arc is evaluated the next word is requested. When the parsing
starts the first word is read in initializing the input buffer.

A buffer is realized as a list. Each element represents a token. To
maintain the buffer, two pointers are used. One which refers to the
whole list of tokens and one which refers to the last one. The second
pointer takes the role of the '*' variable. Some additional functions
are necessary to create buffers and pointers and retrieve information
from a token.

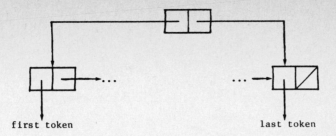

Figure 5.5: The Input Buffer with Pointers. First Version

The definition of the transition function(s) TO1 has to be changed. If
NOMOVEFLAG=NIL it isn't sufficient any longer to decrease the variable
SYNTAX. Instead the next token should be requested. If it is read in
the input buffer is updated and parsing continues.

This will work well as long as no backtracking occurs. In such a case
the buffer must be shrinked if consuming arcs were evaluated on the
aborted path, i.e. the same tokens must be requested again if the parser finds a successful alternative with other consuming arcs. To avoid
this a second set of pointers is defined.

The first of these new pointers refers to the whole buffer, too. But
the second points to the actual token, i.e. to that token which should
be taken by the next consuming arc. To support backtracking means now
to create copies of these pointers every time TO1 is called with NO-
MOVEFLAG=NIL. The user is only requested to give the next token if the
actual token is identical to the last one in the buffer.

The necessary changes to the interpreter are in the monitor and in the
transition function. In the monitor additional variables must be defined and the buffer must be initialized with the first token. In TO1
a function READ-IN is used to get the next actual token.

```
(DE PARSE1 (MACHINE)
   (LET (INPUTBUFFER (INPUT-BUFFER MACHINE)
         OUTPUTBUFFER (OUTPUT-BUFFER MACHINE))
      (INIT-READ-IN INPUTBUFFER)
      (LET (STATE (GET-INIT-STATE MACHINE)
            POP-STACK (LIST (CONS (LIST T)
                                  (GET-PHRASETYPE MACHINE)))
            SYNTAX (COPY-BUFFER INPUTBUFFER)
```

```
        CSYNTAX (CURR-SYNTAX INPUTBUFFER)
        * (CURR-WORD INPUTBUFFER)
        ** NIL
        ATN-CL 1
        REG-STACK NIL)
    (LABEL (TO (GET 'TO1 'TOP-DOWN/DEPTH-FIRST))
        (CATCH (CATCH (TO1 STATE T)
                      EVAL-ARC)
            TOP-LEVEL)))))
```

Figure 5.6: The Monitor. Third Version

```
(LAMBDA (STATE NOMOVEFLAG)
    (COND
        [NOMOVEFLAG (SETQ * (CURR-WORD SYNTAX))
                    (EVAL-STATE STATE)]
        [T (LET (SYNTAX (READ-IN))
            (LET (CSYNTAX (CURR-SYNTAX SYNTAX)
                * (CURR-WORD SYNTAX)
                ** NIL)
            (EVAL-STATE STATE)))]))
```

Figure 5.7: The Standard Transition Function. Third Version

The next figure shows how the pointer into the buffer are organized.

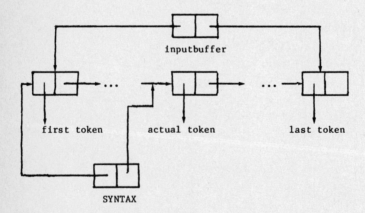

Figure 5.8: The Input Buffer with Pointers. Second Version

The following figure shows the code for the functions which initialize and maintain the buffer. There is only one function which is machine dependent. To implement it, you have to know the character code for carriage return and line feed. For the pointers into the buffer the LISP primitive TCONC is used [interlisp].

```
(DE INIT-READ-IN ()
  (MSG T "give the first word:")
  (SETQ INPUTBUFFER
        (TCONC NIL
               (LET (FIRST-WORD (READ))
                    (GETLEXENTRY FIRST-WORD)))))
(DE READ-IN ()
  (COND
     [(EQ (CDR INPUTBUFFER)
          (CDR SYNTAX))
      (TCONC INPUTBUFFER (READ-WORD))
      (COPY-BUFFER INPUTBUFFER)]
     [T (CONS (CAR INPUTBUFFER)
              (CDDR SYNTAX))]))
(DE READ-WORD ()
  (MSG T "next word:")
  (CLEARBUF)
  (SELECTQ (TYIPEEK)
           [ <CR> (MSG T "end of input detected." T)
                  "END-OF-STRING"]
           (GETLEXENTRY (READ))))
```

Figure 5.9: The Read Functions

The variable INPUTBUFFER is used free in these functions. Its value is always two pointers into the input. The same is true for the variable SYNTAX. The function READ-IN returns always two new pointers which will be the new value for SYNTAX in TO1. The function GETLEXENTRY returns a list. The first element is the word given as its argument. All other elements are lexical entries. This function must be written by the user of this ATN system.

5.4 Looking Ahead

After changing the read of the ATN interpreter it is possible to define the behaviour of LOOKAHEADW and LOOKAHEADC. Both have to inspect the next token which wasn't analyzed until now. It should be sufficient to discuss this only for LOOKAHEADW because it is independent of idiosyncratics of lexical entries.

At first the algorithm seems simple. If the actual token is the last token in the input buffer a new token has to be given by the user. Otherwise the next token to the left of the actual token is inspected. The pointer to the actual token should not be updated. This is the task of a consuming arc.

But this works only correct if the arc in question is a consuming arc. Otherwise the actual token is to be inspected by LOOKAHEADW. Because it will always be evaluated in the scope of an arc LOOKAHEADW can discriminate both situations with the predicate NON-CONSUMING-ARC?.

```
(DEFMACRO LOOKAHEADW (WORDS)
   '(PROGN
      (COND
        [(AND (NOT ,(NON-CONSUMING-ARC? ARC))
              (EQ (CADR INPUTBUFFER)
                  (CADR SYNTAX)))
         (READ-IN)])
      (MEMQ (CAADDR SYNTAX)
            WORDS))
```

Figure 5.10: Looking One Word Ahead

6.0 THE COMPILER

As in every programming language a compiler for ATNs has the purpose to optimize the run time behavior. The design of it is similar to a LISP compiler. Especially it is an incremental compiler in opposition to that described in [Burton 1976]. The target language is LISP which has normally its own compiler. For further improvements a grammar writer may use it to get in two steps machine code.

Because cpu times are relative to a given computer and LISP system a better base for a comparison is the code produced by a compiler. Therefore, some results of the code produced by the compiler are included in this section.

6.1 The Two Steps of Compilation

There are three factors (at least) which make the interpretation process
expansive compared to an aquivalent grammar written immediately in LISP.
First a lot of calls of the LISP interpreter. Second unnecessary CATCHes
and third unnecessary LAMBDA-environments to isolate side effects.

The compiler does something for the first factor and all for the others.
This is done in a first step. The result is efficient code according to
the ATN language. But there are places were redundant LISP code may be
produced. The compiler takes care only for one situation. This is based
on the obversation that in all of our applications other situations are
so seldom that it isn't worthwile to optimize them.

A third step can be done independently to produce machine code, i.e. to
call the LISP compiler with a state. A drawback of this approach is that
the only ATN constructs which this ATN compiler can handle are states
and arcs. More should be gained by network or grammar oriented compiler.

On the other hand an incremental compiler has one advantage. It isn't
necessary to recompile the whole grammar when only minor modifications
on some states are done. Because in our projects the construction of experimental parsers is the main task this aspect has a higher priority
than producing the most efficient compilation.

6.2 Compiling Arcs

As in the interpreter every arc type has its own compiling specialist.
These specialists are called by the top level function COMPILE-ARC. But
most of them doesn't know anything about idiosyncratics of an arc type.
These are already encoded in the arc specialists for the interpreter.
It seemed very cumbersome to repeat that knowledge in the compiling spe-
cialists.

Nevertheless, COMPILE-ARC must know the compiling specialists. To ensure that new arc types can be handled by the compiler without any modifications of it COMPILE-ARC computes the name of the specialist. This
name must obey the following convention. It has to start with the string
COMPILE- and end with the arc type, e.g. the specialist for WORD is COM-
PILE-WORD.

In case that an unknown arc type is encountered the compiler doesn't
break down. It uses then a conservative strategy to compile that arc

without trying to optimize it. Both features should ensure that this
compiler is quite robust against modifications of the ATN language by
a user.

```
(DE COMPILE-ARC (ARC)
    (MACROEXPAND
        (LET (ARC-COMPILE-FN (INTERN (STRING-APPEND
                                        "COMPILE-"
                                        (ARCTYPE ARC))))
            (COND
                [(FNTYP ARC-COMPILE-FN)
                 (FUNCALL ARC-COMPILE-FN ARC)]
                [T (LET (SIDE-EFFECTS? T ABORTS? T)
                    (CATCHIFY? (ISOLATE? (LIST ARC))))])))))
```

Figure 6.1: Compilation of Arcs

The specialists for those arcs which are defined as macros have the
following simple definition.

```
(DE COMPILE-<arctype> (ARC)
    (ISOLATE-CATCHIFY? (LIST ARC)))
```

Figure 6.2: Specialist for an Arc Defined as Macro

This definition assumes that the expanded code of this arc will be the
most optimal one according to a specific arc. A general assumption is
that every arc is given in its original form to COMPILE-ARC. (In LISP
there is the possibility of destructive macros. See Appendix A.) Only
then it is guaranteed that possible side effects and VERIFY actions are
detected.

The result in both alternatives in COMPILE-ARC is the original arc with
some additions according to the value of SIDE-EFFECTS? and ABORT?. This
code is then given as argument to MACROEXPAND. This function expands all
macro calls. That will produce similar code to the expansion schemes
given in chapter 4.

6.3   Checking for Side Effects

Besides these arc specialists there is one specialist which knows what
constructs in the ATN language creates side effects. It is responsible
to detect VERIFY actions. In such a case a CATCH must be used where the

first argument is the code for the given arc. It also searches for any SETR action inside of an arc. If one occurs a LAMBDA environment must be created to isolate the setting of registers.

The name of this specialist is CODE-CHECKER. It uses two flags ABORTS? and SIDE-EFFECTS? as free variables. They are initialized with NIL. If ABORTS? has the value T after CODE-CHECKER is finished, the given arc has a VERIFY action. The function CATCHIFY? will then produce code of the form

    (CATCH <arc code> EVAL-ARC)

If SIDE-EFFECTS? has value T one of the register setting actions occured on the arc. In this case the function ISOLATE? will produce code of the form

    (LET (REG-STACK REG-STACK) <arc code>)

The function CODE-CHECKER uses a specialist TRAVERSE for analyzing the list of actions on an arc. TRAVERSE knows where in a given piece of LISP code it should look at to detect side effects. Only those side effects according to the definition of the ATN language can be found.

If a grammar writer enlarges the set of such side effect producing functions s/he has to change the definition of TRAVERSE as well. Otherwise the compiler may not produce the desired code.

If TRAVERSE detects either a VERIFY or a register setting action it will call the function NOTE-CODE with two arguments. They are either T or NIL. If the first is T the flag SIDE-EFFECTS? is set. Respectively, the variable ABORT? is set if the second argument is T. After that NOTE-CODE will check if both flags are now T which means the most complicated case occured.

Further analysis by TRAVERSE can not change the situation therefore NOTE-CODE notifies CODE-CHECKER that the code is checked. If one of the flags is NIL, then TRAVERSE is forced to step through the next piece of code.

There is one function which combines a call to CODE-CHECKER, ISOLATE?, and CATCHIFY?. This is CATCHIFY-ISOLATE? used by the arc specialists above. The definitions of ISOLATE? and CATCHIFY? are given in the next figure. ISOLATE? must be called with a list containing the arc as its only element because this list will be spliced in.

```
(DE ISOLATE? (CODE)
    (SELECTQ SIDE-EFFECTS?
        [T '(LET (REG-STACK REG-STACK)
                ,@CODE)]
        '(PROGN ,@CODE)))

(DE CATCHIFY? (CODE)
    (SELECTQ ABORTS?
        [T '(CATCH ,CODE EVAL-ARC)]
        CODE))
```

Figure 6.3: Isolating Side Effects and VERIFY Actions

6.4 Compiling States

To compile a single state is now a very simple task. Compile each arc
in the arcset of the given state, make a sequence of the code, optimize
it, and store it as function definition for that state. The following
figure gives the basic definition for this state compiling function.

```
(DE COMPILE-STATE1 (NAME ARCS)
    (SETF (GET NAME 'EXPR)
        (LET (CODE '(LAMBDA NIL
                        (PROGN ,@(FOR (ARC IN ARCS)
                                    (SAVE (COMPILE-ARC ARC)))
                        )))
            (SIMPLIFY CODE)
            CODE)))
```

Figure 6.4: Compiling a Single State. First Version

This situation is complicated because there might be somewhere in the
grammar a VERIFY action where the second argument is just this state
name. In this case the complete code must be embedded in a CATCH with
the state name as its label. The function DIRECTED-BACKUP? will produce
this code exactly in that case.

```
(DE DIRECTED-BACKUP? (NAME ARC-CODE)
    (COND
        [(GET NAME 'DIRECTED-BACKUP)
         '(CATCH ,ARC-CODE , NAME)]
        [T ARC-CODE]))
```

```
(DE COMPILE-STATE1 (NAME ARCS)
   (SETF (GET NAME 'EXPR)
         (LET (CODE '(LAMBDA NIL
                      ,(DIRECTED-BACKUP? NAME
                        '(PROGN ,@(FOR (ARC IN
                                       (GETOUTARCS NAME))
                                      (DO      (COMPILE-ARC
                                      ARC)))))))
            (SIMPLIFY CODE)
            CODE)))
```

Figure 6.5: Compiling a State. Second Version

6.5 Optimizing Code

The ATN compiler described so far will produce fairly optimal code.
There is only one type of inefficiency which can't be avoided by it.
At several places it is assumed that the resulting LISP code is a sequence of function calls. Such a sequence has to be written in LISP
using the function PROGN. It is similar to the BLOCK statement in other
languages. The syntactic form is

   (PROGN <s1> <s2> ... <sn>)

There are some situations where such a PROGN call is redundant, e.g. if
one of the function calls <si> themselves are a PROGN.

   (PROGN <s1> ... (PROGN <s11> ... <sn1>) ... <sn>)

This is semantically equivalent to

   (PROGN <s1> ... <s11> ... <sn1> ...<sn>)

The function SIMPLIFY analyzes a piece of LISP code looking for PROGNs.
It is finds one it tries to optimize the arguments according to the
patterns in the following figure. The value of SIMPLIFY is NIL. It does
it's job by changing the list representation of the code, i.e. it uses
RPLACA and RPLACD.

1. (PROGN <s1>)   ==>   <s1>
2. (PROGN <s1> ... (PROGN <s11> ... <sn1>) ... <sn>)
    ==>
    (PROGN <s1> ...<s11> ... <sn1> ... <sn>)

```
3.  (LAMBDA <vars><s1> ... (PROGN <s11> ... <sn1>) ... <sn>)
    ==>
    (LAMBDA <vars><s1> ... <s11> ... <sn1> ... <sn>)
```

Figure 6.6: PROGN Patterns for SIMPLIFY

These patterns occur quite frequently. As shown above some arcs expand
to a PROGN, e.g. SEEK and JUMP arcs. On the other hand the general scheme
for compiling the arcs of a state is

```
(PROGN <compiled 1. arc>
       <compiled 2. arc>
       ...
       <compiled n. arc>)
```

In this case the expansion of a SEEK or JUMP arc to a PROGN matches the
second pattern in the above figure. But there are cases where this PROGN
must remain, e.g. if a VERIFY action appears on such an arc this PROGN
will be the first argument of a CATCH and is therefore not redundant.
The next figure gives the result of compiling one subnet of the grammar G3.

```
(DEFUN Y1 NIL
    ((LAMBDA (REG-STACK)
        (AND
          [MEMQ * '(A)]
          [PROGN (SETQ ** (GETF NF))
                 (**SETR** 'N (1+ ( **GETR** 'N ATN-CL)))
                 (TO1  'Y2 NIL) ))
      REG-STACK))
  (DEFUN Y2 NIL
    (AND
      [MEMQ * '(B)]
      [PROGN (SETQ ** (GETF NF))
             (TO1 'Y4 NIL)])
    ((LAMBDA (REG-STACK)
        (**SETR** 'N (1+ ATN-CL) ( **GETR** 'N ATN-CL))
        ((LAMBDA (ATN-CL POP-STACK)
             (TO1  'Y1 T))
         (1+ ATN-CL)
         (CONS '(P ( **SETR** 'N ATN-CL *)
                   (TO1 'Y3 T))
               POP-STACK)))
      REG-STACK))
```

```
(DEFUN Y3 NIL
   (AND
      [MEMQ * '(B)]
      [PROGN (SETQ ** (GETF NF))
             (TO1 'Y4 NIL)]))

(DEFUN Y4 NIL
   (AND
      [MEMQ (CAR (TOP-OF POP-STACK)) '(P)]
      [(LAMBDA (ATN-CL POP-STACK REG-STACK ACTIONS *)
            (AND
               [TERMINATED?]
               [TERMINATE-PARSE *])
            (EVALN ACTIONS))
         (1- ATN-CL)
         (CDR POP-STACK)
         (CLEAR-REGS ATN-CL REG-STACK)
         (CDR (TOP-OF POP-STACK))
         (**GETR** 'N ATN-CL)]))
```

Figure 6.7: Compiled Subnet of Grammar G3

As stated above all of explicit calls to the LISP interpreter are removed but the one in Y4 (implicit in EVALN). There the compilation of
the SEND arc resulted to an AND with a LAMBDA expression somewhere.
This gives the appropriate bindings for the calling SEEK arc. The AC-
TIONS variable is bound to the post actions of such a SEEK arc. The
reason is that at compile time the compiler can't tell which SEEK arc
will call this subnet. Therefore, the post actions are saved at run time
on the POP-STACK. The function EVALN will evaluate them by calling the
LISP interpreter.

It is obvious that all information about the arc type from which the
code was produced is lost. Similar each register operation is replaced
by a call to **SETR** or **GETR**. Therefore, the debugger can't trace
which arc is used during a parse.

Further, improvement could be gained by a network or grammar compiler.
There it would be possible to remove calls to EVAL-STATE. This will require a redefinition of the transition function(s). But in our more experimental oriented parsers the result of the state compiler is sufficient. As it was stated above it allows easy recompilation when parts
of the grammar are changed.

7.0 DATA STRUCTURES

In chapter 3 some examples of ATN grammars were given. While the graphical representation was very similar to those given in other publications about ATNs nothing was said how all these ATN objects are represented internally. This is the aim of this chapter.

7.1 Representation of States and Arcs

As was shown in the discussion of the interpreter the arcs are evaluated as LISP functions. Therefore, they must be represented according
to the syntax of function calls in LISP. This is achieved automatically
when the diagrams are transformed to a linear representation by the
user.

For reasons discussed in the next chapter a state is not realized by
some data structure which associates the name of the state with the set
of leaving arcs (called outarcs furtheron). In addition the set of in-
coming arcs (called inarcs) is associated with it.

Normally a state is defined using the function ARCSET. It takes two arguments. The first is the name of the state and the second is the list
of outarcs. The user has not to know anything about which arcs will
lead to this state. This is computed by ARCSET.

The algorithm for doing that is very simple. ARCSET looks in each outarc if there is a destination (depending on the arc type). If the destination is already a defined state the arc under investigation is added
to the inarcs of it. Otherwise a state is first created with the name
given in the destination.

Because an arc contains only information about its destination but nothing about its beginning the set of inarcs are represented as an association list. Given a state X its set of inarcs is an association list containing all arcs pointing to X. Every entry in this association list
consists of a state and exactly those inarcs leaving this state.

Every arc is represented exactly once. Therefore, the 'set of outarcs'
and the 'set of inarcs' hold only pointers to the representation of
some arcs. Assume one follows a pointer out of the set of inarcs to
some arc and changes this arc. Then the changed arc will be found following the appropriate pointer out of the set of outarcs. The next fi-

gure demonstrates this kind of forward and backward linking for the grammar G2.

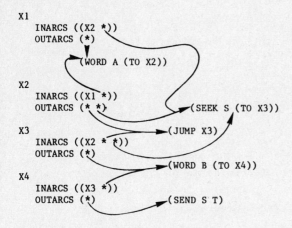

Figure 7.1: Representation of Grammar G2. First Version

While reading this diagram you have to keep in mind that all state names themselves are pointers to one place, e.g. if you are in the arc (WORD A (TO X2)) it is possible to get the inarcs of X2 and therefore to come back to X1. This is in principle enough to move with an editor from state to state forward or backward.

But even a better situation can be achieved if instead of a pointer to a state name the complete state is present. This will result in a circular list structure. If you have one state you have the whole grammar. The next figure makes this a little bit clearer. The data structure used to represent a state is a list with a fixed number of elements. The general form of such a list is:

    (<state name> <outarcs> <inarcs> <network> <phrasetypes>)

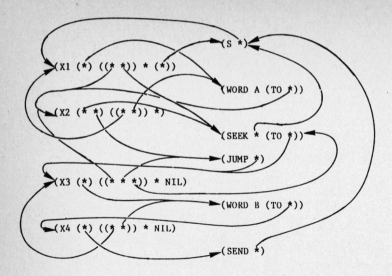

Figure 7.2: Representation of Grammar G2. Second Version

What is missing in both figures is the exact representation of the other
ATN objects in a grammar. It is obvious that searching a state in the
former representation means to follow two different kinds of pointers
while in the latter one only one kind of pointer is used.

The circular representation works only when at the same time the function TO is changed to get the next state. In the following we describe
in more detail the former representation. It proposes a constructor for
states, selectors for parts of information contained in a state, predi-
cates, and updaters.

A state is represented by a LISP atom whose print name is the name of
the state. The sets of inarcs and outarcs are associated via the property list of that atom. When we talk of a state we mean normally this
atom together with it's property list. The constructor used by a grammar
writer is ARCSET.

```
(DE ARCSET (STATE OUTARCS)
  (OR
    [STATEP STATE]
    [INIT-STATE STATE]))
```

```
      (FOR [ARC IN OUTARCS]
            [DO (ADD-OUTARC-TO-STATE STATE ARC)])
      STATE)
```

Figure 7.3: The User Constructor for States

The function STATEP is a predicate for states. If the given state in
ARCSET is yet no state the function INIT-STATE creates an empty state.
Then the OUTARCS are added using the updater ADD-OUTARC-TO-STATE, i.e.
ARCSET creates only new states if necessary otherwise it is an updater
for already defined states. The 'real' constructor is INIT-STATE.

```
  (DEFMACRO INIT-STATE (STATE)
      '(PROGN (PUSH DEFINED-STATES ,STATE)
              (INIT-INARCS ,STATE)
              (INIT-OUTARCS ,STATE)))

  (DE INIT-INARCS (STATE)
    (OR
      [GETINARCS STATE]
      [PUTPROP STATE NIL 'INARCS])
    STATE)

  (DE INIT-OUTARCS (STATE)
    (OR
      [GETOUTARCS STATE]
      [PUTPROP STATE NIL 'OUTARCS])
    STATE)

  (DE STATEP (THING)
    (AND
      [MEMQ 'OUTARCS (GETPROPLIST THING)]
      [MEMQ 'INARCS (GETPROPLIST THING]))

  (DE GETOUTARCS (STATE)
    (GET STATE 'OUTARCS))

  (DE GETINARCS (STATE FROM-STATE)
    (COND
      [(NULL FROM-STATE) (GET STATE 'INARCS)]
      [T (ASSQ FROM-STATE (GET STATE 'INARCS))]))
```

Figure 7.4: Constructor, Selectors, and Predicate for States

The selector GETINARCS serves for two purposes. One is to get the complete set of inarcs, i.e. the association list. The other is to get an entry in this list. Therefore it takes two arguments. The second is optional and gives the state name from which the inarcs should come.

The next functions realizes the algorithm mentioned above. It is triggered with ADD-OUTARC-TO-STATE. It takes into account all arc types given in chapter 2 and creates if necessary new states. The function MODIFY-INARCS does the main work. It uses the function INSERT-INARC to update the set of inarcs for a given state.

```
(DE ADD-OUTARC-TO-STATE (STATE OUTARC)
  (AND
    [MEMQ (ARCTYPE OUTARC) META-ARCS]
    [FOR [ARC IN (REST OUTARC)]
         [DO (MODIFY-INARCS (DESTINATION ARC) ARC STATE)]])
  (INSERT-OUTARC STATE OUTARC)
  (MODIFY-INARCS (DESTINATION OUTARC) OUTARC STATE)
  (GETOUTARCS STATE))

(DE MODIFY-INARCS (STATE INARC FROM-STATE)
  (COND
    [(MEMQ (ARCTYPE INARC) META-ARCS) NIL]
    [(NOT STATE) NIL]
    [(OR [STATEP STATE]
         [ARCSET STATE NIL])
     (AND [EQ 'SEEK
             (ARCTYPE INARC)]
          [INSERT-INARC (SUBNET INARC)
                        FROM-STATE
                        (GETINARCS (SUBNET INARC)
                                   FROM-STATE)])
     (INSERT-INARC STATE FROM-STATE (GETINARCS STATE
                                               FROM-STATE))]
  ) )
(DE INSERT-INARC (STATE FROM-STATE INARCS)
  (COND
    [(NULL INARCS)
     (ADDPROP STATE (LIST FROM-STATE INARC) 'INARCS)]
    [T (RPLACD INARCS
               (CONS INARC (CDR INARCS)))
```

```
(GETINARCS STATE)])))
```

Figure 7.5: Creating Forward and Backward Links between States

The function MODIFY-INARCS takes as arguments the three parts which con-
stitutes an arc in a diagram. The state to which the arc leads, the arc
itself, and the state from which the arc comes. MODIFY-INARCS does only
any changes if the given arc is not a meta arc and the end state of the
arc is not NIL. The latter case occurs for SEND arcs. If necessary the
end state is initialized, i.e. it is created, and then the arc is added
via INSERT-INARC to the association list.

While there is no constructor for arcs some selectors exist which are
used in the functions described above. ARCTYPE gets the type of a given
arc, ARCACTIONS the actions, ARCTEST the special test, DESTINATION the
end state of the arc (if there is any), and SUBNET gives the initial
state for a subnet called by a SEEK arc.

7.2 Representation of Networks and Grammars

Networks and grammars are in some sense very similar because they group
smaller parts of an ATN together. Therefore, only networks are described
in more detail. The same line of discussion applies to grammars.

A network is also like states represented by a LISP atom and a property
list of this atom. Associated with a network name is the list of states
in this network and the grammar name of which it is an element. The following functions handle networks. The constructor NETWORK, the predicate
NETWORKP, the updater ADD-STATE-TO-NETWORK and ADD-NETWORK-TO-GRAMMAR,
and the selectors GETSTATES and GETNETWORK.

```
(DE NETWORK (NAME STATES)
   (OR [NETWORKP NAME]
       [PUSH DEFINED-NETWORKS NAME])
   (FOR [STATE IN STATES]
        [DO (ADD-STATE-TO-NETWORK STATE NAME)])
   NAME)

(DEFMACRO ADD-STATE-TO-NETWORK (STATE NETWORK)
     '(PROGN (OR [MEMQ ,STATE (GETSTATES ,NETWORK)]
                 [ADDPROP ,NETWORK ,STATE 'STATES])
             (PUTPROP ,STATE ,NETWORK 'NETWORK)))
```

```
(DE GETSTATES (NETWORK-OR-GRAMMAR)
  (COND
    [(GRAMMARP NETWORK-OR-GRAMMAR)
     (APPLY 'NCONC
            (FOR [NETWORK IN (GETNETWORKS
                                   NETWORK-OR-GRAMMAR)]
                 [SAVE (GETSTATES NETWORK)]))]
    [T (GET NETWORK-OR-GRAMMAR 'STATES)]))

(DE GETNETWORK (STATE)
  (GET STATE 'NETWORK))
```

Figure 7.6: The Functions for Networks

As the function GETSTATES shows it is possible to pass the information along the hierarchy state, network, grammar up and down.

The constructor NETWORK is in some sense very primitive. The reason is that during the definition of states all information is present to update the list of states belonging to a network. This would require a more complicated scheme because it is possible to start with the definition of a state which is not the initial state of a network. As long as the network for a state is unknown some dummy network has to collect all states which are defined on pathes emerging from this state.

With the network structure given here it is possible to group arbitrary states together. This is alright when the grammar writer doesn't try tricks. Also in some experimental situations it is more convenient to define networks in this way, e.g. one wants to save onto a file only those states of a network which are debugged.

7.3 Representation of Phrasetypes

The datastructure for a phrasetype connects it with a state which serves as initial state for that phrasetype. Creating one means also to associate the state with the name of this phrasetype. It is realized also with property lists.

```
(DE PHRASETYPE (NAME STATE)
  (PUTPROP NAME STATE 'INIT-STATE)
  (OR [STATEP STATE]
      [INIT-STATE STATE])
```

```
     (ADDPROP STATE NAME 'PHRASETYPES)
     (PUSH DEFINED-PHRASETYPES NAME)
      NAME)

   (DE GETPHRASETYPE (STATE)
     (GET STATE 'PHRASETYPES))

   (DE GETINITSTATE (PHRASETYPE)
     (GET PHRASETYPE 'INIT-STATE))
```

Figure 7.7: Constructor and Selectors for Phrasetypes

Therefore, the function SUBNET which gets the initial state of a phrasetype mentioned on a SEEK arc is defined as:

```
   (DE SUBNET (ARC)
     (COND
        [(EQ (ARCTYPE ARC) 'SEEK)
         (GETINITSTATE (ARCTEST ARC))]))
```

Figure 7.8: The Function SUBNET for SEEK Arcs

7.4 File Handling for ATN Objects

Both forms of representation require a special file handling. The reason
is, that some substructures have to be EQ, i.e. identical in their address in the work space. If the arcsets of some states are simply written on to a file, this information is lost. A later load of them will
create copies of these substructures.

The standard way out of this situation is to save the appropriate calls
of the constructors. Loading such a file means then to read and evaluate the stored function calls. They will automatically create the desired representations. This simple scheme is only complicated if it is
possible to load parts of a grammar while the complete grammar is already in the work space. In this case they have to be deleted before
they are created via the constructor calls in the file. This is because
the constructors for ATN objects will update an already existing object
instead of creating a new one.

The work horse for saving objects onto a file is ATN-FILE. It takes
three arguments. The first specifies a list of objects (either grammars,
networks, or states). The second is the file name, and the third gives

the name of a printing function. The problem is, if a given object is
the name of a grammar, not only a call to GRAMMAR should be stored on
the file. In addition all networks and states of this grammar should be
saved, too.

The following definition of ATN-FILE uses only one function which is
idiosyncratic to our LISP-system. Its name is IOC and it switches input
and output channels. At the beginning the two calls of IOC direct the
output onto a file and it is not echoed onto the terminal. At the end
they do the inverse. The functions UWRITE and CLOSE are special forms.
In order to call them with the evaluated arguments they must applied to
them.

```
(DE ATN-FILE (OBJECTS FILE PRINT-FN)
  (APPLY 'UWRITE FILE)
  (IOC W) (IOC R)
  (FOR [OBJ IN OBJECTS]
      [DO (COND
            [(STATEP OBJ)]
             (FUNCALL PRINT-FN
                  '(ARCSET ',OBJ ',(GETOUTARCS OBJ)))]
            [T (COND
                 [(NETWORKP OBJ)
                  (FUNCALL PRINT-FN
                       '(NETWORK ',OBJ ',(GETSTATES
                                         OBJ)))]
                 [(GRAMMARP OBJ)
                  (FUNCALL PRINT-FN
                       '(GRAMMAR ',OBJ
                                 ',(GETNETWORKS OBJ)
                                 ',(GETINITSTATE
                                    OBJ)))
                  (FOR [NETWORK IN (GETNETWORKS OBJ)]
                      [DO (FUNCALL PRINT-FN
                             '(NETWORK ',NETWORK
                                       ',(GETSTATES
                                          NETWORK)))])])])
              (NCONC OBJECTS
                  (FOR [STATE IN (GETSTATES OBJ)]
                      [SPLICE
                        (COND
```

```
                              [ (MEMQ STATE OBJ) NIL]
                              [T (LIST STATE)])])))])])
  (PRINT NIL)
  (TERPRI)
  (IOC T) (IOC V)
  (APPLY 'CLOSE (CAR FILE)) )
```

Figure 7.9: The Main Save Function for ATN Objects

With the third argument in ATN-FILE it is possible to use the pretty-
printer. Then the file can be used for a documentation of a grammar.
Loading a file is independent on how its content was produced. The basic version of the load function is shown in the next figure. It simply
reads every expression from a file, evaluates it, and stops, when it
reads a NIL.

```
  (DF LOADG (ARGL)
    (LET (FILE (CAR ARGL))
      (APPLY 'UREAD FILE)
      (IOC Q)
      (LOOP [INITIAL INPUT (READ) OBJECTS NIL]
            [WHILE INPUT]
            [NEXT OBJECTS (CONS (EVAL INPUT) OBJECTS)
                  INPUT (READ) ]
            [RESULT (MSG "the following ATN objects are
                             loaded:" t OBJECTS) ] )
      (FUNCALL 'CLOSE (CAR FILE)) ) )
```

Figure 7.10: The Basic Load Function

As mentioned above this will only work if complete grammars are saved
and loaded. Otherwise, the LOADG function must test if the object read
from the file is already defined. In this case an erasing function de-
letes the existing object. After that the loaded expression is evaluated.

8.0 AN EDITOR FOR ATN DATA STRUCTURES

All ATN objects are represented by means of LISP list structures. Modifying list structures is the main purpose of LISP structure oriented
editors. But using such an editor for ATN objects requires that the

user has to think in terms of internal representation details instead
of his/her problems with an ATN. Therefore, a special purpose editor is
presented in this chapter.

The approach used here requires that it is possible to define arbitrary
new editor commands for the standard LISP editor. If this feature is not
supported by your LISP you can try to modify it. Because every LISP editor has it's own set of basic commands those defined for handling ATN
objects are defined verbally instead of giving their LISP definition.

The representation for ATNs described in the last chapter assumes that
different parts of a grammar are connected via links stored on property
lists. There is a special version of our editor named EDITP to edit property lists. The drawback when calling EDITP with a state is the following. If you want to change the editors attention to another state you
have to leave it and restart it with this new state. But it will not remember that you started editing with another state.

This problem is solved by a monitor function called ATN-EDIT.It keeps
track of which objects were visited during a session and calls EDITP
every time anew when you want to edit another part in a grammar. Of
course, it is possible to start an edit session with a grammar instead
of a single state. In this case as well as for a network, the monitor
waits until you specify a state before calling EDITP.

8.1 A Simple Pretty Printer

While editing a part of a grammar it is very convenient to see these
parts in terms of how we see an ATN grammar. The basic view of it is
that it is a set of networks. Because our LISP doesn't have any graphic
facility we realized only a pseudo graphical representation for states.
But even this turned out to be very helpful in creating and debugging
a grammar.

Grammars and networks are printed in the following way. First the name
of the object is printed. Then in case of a grammar the networks, and
at last the states in a 'graphical' way. The next figure shows such a
pretty print for grammar G3.

Grammar CONTEXTFREE-GRAMMAR consists of the following networks:
(CONTEXTFREE-TOP)
Subnet CONTEXTFREE-TOP consists of the following states:

```
X2-G2:   SEEK S              |  X1-G2  |  WORD A --->   X2-G2

X1-G2:   WORD A --->         |         |  WORD B --->   X4-G2

                             |  X2-G2  |

                             |         |  SEEK S --->   X3-G2

X2-G2:   SEEK S     --->     |  X3-G2  |  WORD B --->   X4-G2

X2-G2:   WORD B     --->     |  X4-G2  |  SEND (S) T
```

Figure 8: A Pretty Print of Grammar G2

The name of a state is placed in the center of a line. On its left are
the state names with arcs leading to it. While on the right, are the
arcs leaving it with their destination. Normally, there is no place in
one line to print the actions of an arc, too. Therefore, they are omis-
sed when pretty printing a state. If you want to see them you have to
specify one of the states 'containing' this arc and direct the attention
of the editor to this arc. In this case the normal LISP pretty printer
is used to print the arc onto the terminal.

8.2   The Basic Edit Commands

As usual there are commands for shifting the attention, modifying a
structure, and others. The modifying commands try to keep the given part
of a grammar consistent. But this aspect is not very elaborated. So there
might be some cases where the editor refuses the execution of a command.

To edit different states it is possible to change the attention with
the command STATE followed by a state name. The actual EDITP will finish.
Then ATN-EDIT tries to find a state with the given name in the structures
associated with the argument of ATN-EDIT. If it is successful, EDITP will
be called again. Similar commands exist to find a network or a grammar.

The user is supported by some commands which modify the arc sets of a
state, i.e. adding or deleting one will cause an updating of other arc
sets. It is only possible to modify the outarcs of a state. The reason
is that the outarcs are evaluated in a sequence by the interpreter.
Therefore the sequence of the arcs is important. But looking into the
inarcs set you might have only incomplete information about the whole
outarcs set of a specific state. In such a case you have to move the
attention to that state first.

Modifying the actions on an arc is done by the ordinary LISP editor com-

mands. Only for replacing a phrasetype on a SEEK or SEND arc must be
done with the command RP. Similar the state name in the TO action or
on a JUMP arc requires a special command RD.

At the moment there are no commands for answering more complex questions
like 'is there a path from state X to state Y?'. Although the information to compute that answer is there, this like other tasks which could
be done by such an editor [Hadden 1977] are postponed into the future.

9.0 DEBUGGING OF GRAMMARS

While developping a grammar it is very important to test the capabilities of it. That is a very similar situation to programming with a standard programming language. Therefore, all known debugging techniques are
applicable. Those described here are a direct result of implementing
the ATN interpreter in LISP, i.e. the idea of the debugging tools for
LISP is used for ATNs.

What follows is a description of the tracing component. It is not interactive. But it is shown how this deficiency can be removed very easily.
It is open to the user to write specialized debugging routines which are
called at defined points during the evaluation process. Nevertheless,
after compiling a state only the call of a state is recognizable, i.e.
arcs and actions are not traceable any longer.

9.1 The Interface to the Interpreter

The key to the understanding of this debugging system is that it is activated due tracing switches. They are frequently tested by the evaluation specialists. If a switch is on the appropriate ATN construct is
'traced'. The tracing is done with the function TRACER. It is called
with three arguments, the trace switch, a trace value, and a sequence
of trace messages.

```
(DEFMACRO-DISPLACE TRACER (TR-FLAG TR-VALUE . TR-MESSAGES)
     '(PROG2 (AND ,TR-FLAG
              [MSG ,@TR-MESSAGES])
          ,TR-VALUE))
```

Figure 9.1: The Basic Tracing Function

The value of TRACER is independent of the state of a given trace switch. It is always the value of its second argument. This makes it possible to use TRACER even in such LISP functions where the continuation of the evaluation depends upon the values of its arguments, e.g. AND, OR, COND.

The trace switches are bound in a monitor function called ATN. All actions are done in its binding environment. They are initialized with T(rue), i.e. everything during a parse is traced. Besides these switches there are some info variables. Their value is a sequence of messages which are printed by the primitive LISP function MSG.

Variable name	Initial value
STATE-TRACE?	T
ARC-TRACE?	T
REG-TRACE?	T
PUSH-TRACE?	T
MOVE-TO-INFO	(T "to state" STATE (T) *)
ARC-INFO	((T) "trying a" (ARCTYPE ARC)"-arc")
SET-REG-INFO	((T) "set register" REGISTER)
PUSH-INFO	((T) "pushing")

Figure 9.2: The Trace Switches and Info Variables

The following changes to the evaluation specialists given in chapter 4 and 5 are necessary. In EVAL-ARC a call to the function ARC-TRACER with T and ARC-INFO as arguments is inserted at the beginning. The EVAL-STATE will now expand to a PROGN were the first statement is a call to STATE-TRACER with T and MOVE-TO-INFO as arguments. The tracing of setting a register is done in SETR-MACRO with a call to REG-TRACER.

A call to TRACER is inserted into SEEK* and SEND* to trace recursive calls of networks. TRACER is called during the expansion of these macros. A similar call is inserted into GETR. The decision where TRACER or specialized functions are used was done at an early point of implementation and is not very consistent.

If one of the switches are off the corresponding construct is not traced during a parse. If one wants to trace only some states or arcs of one specific type you have to use these switches in another way. Because they are lambda variables and evaluated by TRACER, it is possible to assign arbitrary LISP code.

This can be used to realize a more directed trace, e.g. if the value of
STATE-TRACE? is a MEMQ which returns only not-NIL if the actual state
in a grammar is an element of some given list. The same technique is
applicable for the other switches. Therefore, only a comfortable trace
monitor function is necessary which translates commands given by the
user into appropriate bindings of a switch.

9.2. An Example of a Full Trace

The following text is a protocol of a parse with the grammar G3.

Give the first word:

```
A
    to X1-G3                                              A
        X1-G3: trying a SEEK-arc expecting: P             A
                        set register: N
pushing to Y1-G3.                                         A
        Y1-G3: trying a WORD-arc expecting: A             A
                        set register: N
Next word:
B
    to Y2-G3                                              B
        Y2-G3: trying a WORD-arc expecting: B             B
Next word:
C
    to Y4-G3                                              C
        Y4-G3: trying a SEND-arc expecting: (P)           C
                        set register: N
popping.
    to X2-G3                                              C
        X2-G3: trying a WORD-arc expecting: C             C
Next word:
<CR>     ; Carriage Return
end of input detected.
    to X3-G3                                    END-OF-STRING

        X3-G3: trying a WORD-arc expecting: C   END-OF-STRING
        X3-G3: trying a SEND-arc expecting: (S) END-OF-STRING
successful parse.
```

   Figure 9.3: A Trace of a Parse

Similarly failing of an arc is reported as well as backtracking. For the
latter one it is necessary to use a variable BACKTRACE. It is switched
on every time before the function EVAL-STATE returns NIL, i.e. a state
fails and gives back control to an earlier state. In the function EVAL-
ARC is at the beginning a call of TRACER.

```
(TRACER (AND BACKTRACE STATE-TRACE?)
        (SWITCHOFF BACKTRACE)
        "backing up to" STATE))
```

Figure 9.4: Tracing Backtracking

The variable BACKTRACE isn't necessary at all for the interpretation
process.

9.3 Interactive Debugging

Sometimes in the debugging process it is more convenient to interact
with a specific state of evaluation rather than seeing its result on
the terminal. This might be seen as a generalization of the tracing technique described above. Assume that there is an initialization function
which helps to specify at which points in the evaluation such an inter-
action should start. Such a point is called a break point, e.g. one is
introduced in grammar G3 at the state X2-G3.

Then a special interpretation routine takes place every time when the
evaluation encounters X2-G3. At the beginning it prints a message like

    BREAK in state X2-G3

after that the user has the possibility to inspect the actual state of
the interpreter, grammar, register stack, and input buffer. The function
ATN-BREAK-LIST in the next figure is a basic version of such a READ-EVAL-
PRINT loop.

```
(DE ATN-BREAK-LIST NIL
    (LOOP [INITIAL COM (READ)  %VALUE NIL]
          [DO (SELECTQ COM
                  [OK (SETQ COM NIL)]
                  [RETURN (SETQ COM NIL)
                          (SETQ %VALUE (EVAL (READ)))]
                  [ABORT (THROW NIL TOP-LEVEL)]
                  [E (PRINT (EVAL (READ)))]
```

```
[EDIT (FUNCALL 'ATN-EDIT STATE)]
[RESTART (FUNCALL 'THROW NIL (READ))]
[ACF (PP-ATN-ACF STATE)]
[ALTPATH (THROW NIL EVAL-ARC)]
[PS (FUNCALL 'PS STATE)]
...
(MSG T "unknown command" COM))]
        [WHILE COM]
        [RESULT %VALUE] ) )
```

Figure 9.5: A Simple Interpreter for an Interactive Debugger

It uses two auxiliary variables COM and %VALUE. The value of COM is always the name of some command typed in by the user. %VALUE gives the
value with which the break point should be left. (Note: normally this
returned value is ignored by the ATN interpreter.) There are some commands which allow to leave this loop. Some of them set the variable COM
to NIL which is recognized by ATN-BREAK-LIST as a stop signal. Others
reactivate earlier states of a parsing using a THROW to that state.

The commands OK and RETURN will continue the parsing at the break point.
ABORT will end the actual parsing with a failure, while RESTART tries
a new alternative before the state specified as argument to RESTART. The
command ALTPATH will block the actual arc trying an alternative at the
actual state.

The commands ACF (Actual ConFiguration) and PS print the actual bindings
of REG-STACK, POP-STACK, etc. and a state respectively. With EDIT a edit
session is started for the actual state. The command E allows the user
to type in arbitrary LISP code which is evaluated immediately.

A lot of other commands could be introduced, e.g. those which alter the
ACF in the break point. But this makes only sense if there is a tentative evaluation mode [INTERLISP]. To achieve that it is necessary to
isolate every side effect which can occur. In addition this tentative
evaluation has to start inside a CATCH with label TOP-LEVEL. This will
ensure that the evaluation will come back to the break point. Then the
user can decide what to do next.

10.0 CONCLUSION

While the presented ATN system has a lot of advantages there are, of
course, some flaws and possible improvements. These would turn the given
system to a more effective one but will not enlarge the possible applications of ATNs. But recently Woods suggested a new kind of ATNs which
he called cascaded ATNs [Woods 1980]. A realization of this concept may
lead to a new class of parsers based on ATNs. First I will discuss some
possibilities of technical improvements and will turn then to a possible
implementation of cascaded ATNs within the framework of the given interpreter.

10.1 Further Improvements

The metaarc GROUP was introduced to realize determinism. It does so but
it couldn't avoid the overhead of the standard non-determinism strategy,
i.e. the function call of the GROUP arc and the successful chosen arc in
it will remain on the LISP function stack. This, of course, contradicts
the conception of determinism. A way out of that would be if a GROUP is
defined as a macro which expands into a conditional expression as shown
in the next figure.

```
(COND
    [(AND <special test of 1. arc>
          (CATCH (PROGN <actions of 1. arc> T)
                EVAL-ARC))
     (TO <destination of 1. arc>)]
    [(AND <special test for 2. arc>
          (CATCH (PROGN <actions of 2. arc> T)
                EVAL-ARC)
     (TO <destination of 2. arc>)]
    ... )
```

Figure 10.1: Expansion of a GROUP Arc

In this case it isn't necessary to define a deterministic version of TO1.
And only the function call for the destination will remain on the stack.
The backtracking will automatically pass the untried alternatives of
this GROUP arc.

This corresponds neatly to the code produced by compilation of a 'normal'
set of arcs. The difference is first that the compiled arcset is a PROGN

instead of a COND. Second that the actions together with the call of
the destination are included into a PROGN which is the first argument
of a CATCH with label EVAL-ARC. Of course, this second case occurs only
if there is a VERIFY action which can block its own arc.

But this is unnecessary, too. Such a VERIFY action effects only the evaluation of the actions of an arc. There can't be any action in a later
state which is allow to THROW to this arc. Therefore, the following code
should be the result of compiling a nondeterministic set of arcs.

```
(PROGN
  (LETL (REG-STACK REG-STACK)
   (AND <special test of 1. arc>
        (CATCH (PROGN <actions of 1. arc> T)
               EVAL-ARC))
   (TO1 <destination of 1. arc> <nomoveflag of 1. arc>))
  (LETL (REG-STACK REG-STACK)
   (AND <special test of 2. arc>
        (CATCH (PROGN <actions of 2. arc> T)
               EVAL-ARC))
   (TO1 <destination of 2. arc> <nomoveflag of 2. arc>))
  ... )
```

Figure 10.2: An Improved Compilation of Arcsets

Of course, the code given in figure 10.2 is maximal in the sense that
this will only occur if on every arc there is a VERIFY and register setting action. Otherwise the CATCH or the LETL are omissable. In principle
it is only necessary to have a selector which extracts the actions of an
arc and its destination seperately. But this is more complicated because
the CATCH resulting from a VERIFY, which forces a different state to
fail, should include the destination as well as the actions.

In general the parsing strategy of this interpreter is relative fixed.
Only with metaarcs it is possible to switch between different ones. A
closer look shows that there are two places instead of one where the
strategy is manifested. One is, of course, the transition function. The
other one is the FOR construct in EVAL-STATE. Here is the place where it
is stated that the outarcs of a state are evaluated in a given sequence.

With the actual interpreter it isn't possible to change that. But there
are a lot of phenomena in natural languages which suggest that this is

a much too rigorous approach, e.g. in English it is very unlikely that
an arbitrary number of adjectives proceed a noun. After one or two adjectives encountered in the input the expectation that a third one will
appear is less than that the noun will come.

But with the normal constructs in ATNs it is only possible to block an
arc depending of accumulated information during a parse. It is not possible to change the sequence of expectations at a state dynamically. One
possible solution is mentioned by in [Kerp 1979] where the design of an
interpreter is presented which is closer to that of a GSP [Kaplan 1973].

The idea there is to create a new task when a state is evaluated. This
task will have the outarcs of the state. If this is a copied sequence,
then this task can modify it without changing the original order in the
state. This might lead to a new view of what states are in an ATN. On
one hand, they are data structures which could be created and modified.
On the other hand, they are processes which create and schedule tasks.
This view is implicit in the compiler. Because the result of compiling
a state is that the state is now a function which may be evaluated at
any point in an arbitrary program.

10.2 Cascaded ATNs

What follows is a short characterization of cascaded ATNs and the discussion of an implementation. Basicly a cascaded ATN consists of a sequence of different ATNs. They are connected via buffers, i.e. each ATN
has one 'lower neighbor' and one 'higher neighbour'. A lower ATN can
TRANSMIT some tokens into the inputbuffer of its higher neighbour.

There is one lowest ATN which receives its input from some other device
(terminal, file, etc.). Each ATN in such a cascade is responsible for
some subtask which is more than a subnet in ordinary ATNs, e.g. one ATN
captures morphology, while the next one is a syntax ATN, followed by a
semantic and pragmatic ATN. Each ATN decides for its own when to TRANS-
MIT a token to the next higher one, i.e. each level in the cascade can
run for a while until it has some confidence about its parsing result.
Only then it hands over the control to the next level.

Recently I have implemented an interpreter for cascaded ATNs [Christal-
ler 1981]. This interpreter is quite different from the one presented
here. It has an explicit stack for providing backtracking in each level
of such a cascade. And a second stack for backtracking in the cascade

as a whole. The reason was that the 'local' backtracking had to look
with which configuration a single level was activated by another one.
If it turned out to backtrack beneath that point it had to activate a
backtrack in the cascade. This is a point not mentioned in [Woods 1980].

But the drawback was that such an ATN couldn't be compiled using the
techniques described in chapter 6. Therefore, another interpreter is
necessary. To think in terms of cascaded ATNs a TRANSMIT from a lower
to a higher level means the following. The actual arc has to give the
control to last activated configuration of the higher level. And to
store away its own actual configuration for later processing.

But this means to create a continuation for the current process, and
calling the higher level with that continuation. If the higher level
needs some more input it uses that continuation to reactivate the lower
level, i.e. each level in a cascade has two possible continuations. One
in the case that it TRANSMITs something to a higher level. A second one
if it wants to read new input.

On the other hand the complete knowledge about an ATN configuration is
stored as values of lambda variables. In LISP there is one possibility
to create continuations. Such a continuation is called a FUNARC or
CLOSURE [Steele 1978]. When a level in a cascade wants to activate another one, it simply sets a flag. This flag signals if the request is
a TRANSMIT or a read.

The transition function must be sensitive to the value of this flag. If
it is set, it has to create a closure representing the actual configuration. According to the type of request, it activates another level in
the cascade. This will be given as one of the continuations of the actual level. Because a closure is a functional object for LISP it just
evaluates this continuation. With this technique the problem of the in-
terference of local and global backtracking mentioned above is avoided.

This is the principal idea for implementing an interpreter for cascaded
ATNs which may be compiled by the given compiler. There remain some problems according the connection between different levels in a cascade.
One solution to them is to maintain for each level an input and output
buffer with the same organization as described in chapter 5. But these
buffers are shared by neighboured ATNs, i.e. the output buffer of the
lowest ATN is the input buffer for the next one etc. The input buffer

for the lowest ATN is the terminal or a file and the output buffer of
the highest level, too.

It is planned to use cascaded ATNs as a formalism to describe dialogue
models. This application in mind it will be necessary to modify the
sketchy version above. One obvious problem is that the length of parts
of a dialogue which is covered by each level is different. Assume that
there is an ATN cascade where the lowest level is a lexicographical parser for words or morphemes. The second level a phrase oriented syntax
ATN. The third an ATN to find the semantics of a single utterance. And
at the top a dialogue grammar which parses sequences of speech acts
[Christaller, Metzing 1982].

A solution to this problem together with the possibility to use at least
the dialogue grammar also for generating will create a new class of parsers. The main advantage should be that they have a uniform data structure and well defined interactions between different kind of parsing
tasks.

APPENDIX A

This appendix serves as a reference to those LISP constructs used in
the implementation which are to may knowledge not standard or not available in other LISP dialects than the one I used.

BACKQUOTE
    A very simple pattern matcher. Described in more detail in [LISPMA-
    CHINE]. Assume that the variable B has as its value the list (X Y Z).
    Then:
    - '(A B C) will produce the same list (A B C)
    - '(A ,B C) will produce the list (A (X Y Z) C)
    - '(A ,@B C) will produce the list (A X Y Z C)
      The value of B is 'spliced' into the list.

CATCH and THROW
    A simple version of an escape operator [Reynolds 1972].
    (CATCH <s-expr> <label>) is equivalent to <s-expr> as long as no
    (THROW <value> <Label>) is evaluated. But if so the first argument
    of THROW is evaluated in the actual environment and then this value
    will be that of the CATCH. The <label> argument ensures that a THROW
    can 'select' its CATCH.

DEFMACRO

defines macros [LISPMACHINE]. The syntax is

    (DEFMACRO <name> <pattern> . <body>)

The <pattern> may be an arbitrary expression. Each atom in it serves
as a variable which can be used inside of <body>. When the macro is
called its actual arguments are matched against the <pattern> which
produces the binding. The rest is like in every macro (see there).

FOR

A macro which unifies some of the traditional MAP-functions in LISP
[Charniak et. al. 1980].

    (FOR [<var1> IN <list1>]
         [<var2> IN <list2>]
          ...
         [<keyword> . <body>])

steps with <var1> simultaneous through the lists <list1>. The body
is evaluated at each step. The <keyword> determines what to do with
the values of this evaluations.

functional arguments, FUNARC, closure

LISP is a programming language which uses dynamic binding for its
variables. This caused the so-called FUNARG problem [Moses 1970]. A
solution to that in MacLISP is the closure construct. Essentially it
is a functional object which contains the binding of its free variables at definition time (lexical binding). Such an object can be passed
around as argument or value to resp. of other functions.

LETL and LET

is a macro for a lambda expression applied to some arguments.

    (LETL (<var1> <val1> <var2> <val2> ...) . <body>)

is equivalent to

    ((LAMBDA (<var1> <var2> ...) . <body>) <val1> <val2> ...)

in LETL all variables are evaluated in parallel while in LET they
are evaluated in a sequence.

LOOP

A macro for writing iterative code in a structured way [Charniak et.
al. 1980].

    (LOOP [INITIAL <var1> <init1> <var2> <init2> ...]
          [<keyword1> <s-expr1>]
           ...
          [RESULT <value>])

macros

Thoroughly discussed in [Allen 1978] [Charniak et. al. 1980]
[Winston, Horn 1981]. A macro call evaluates twice. The first time
is called the expansion of the macro. This is done by evaluating the
body of the macro definition. The second one is the evaluation of the
value achieved by the expansion. This is done outside of the bindings
of the body. Most macros are written in such a way that they are ex-
pandable at 'definition' time or 'compile' time instead of 'run' time.

Object oriented programming

This programming technique is based on work done in the development
of SMALLTALK [Kay, A. 1972], ACTORS [Hewitt 1977], CSSA [Raulefs 1979].
As shown by Steele and Sussman [Steele et. al. 1975] a 'correct' implementation of the lambda calculus could serve as a model for these
languages. A similar approach is supported in LISPMACHINE LISP by its
flavor system [Christaller 1981b].

SETF

A macro which unifies all of the 'assigning' operators in LISP [LISP-
MACHINE] [Charniak et. al. 1980]. E.g.
- (SETF <var> <value>) assigns <value> to the variable <var>.
- (SETF (<selector> <data structure>) <new>) updates that part of
<data structure> which is accessible with the given <selector> func-
tion.

TCONC

This is a function borrowed from INTERLISP. It creates and maintains
list pointers. Such a pointer is initialized by
    (SETF <pointer> (TCONC NIL <first element>))
The CAR of <pointer> gives the complete list while CDR of <pointer>
gives the last element of the list attached by TCONC.
    (TCONC <pointer> <added element>)
will add a new element at the end of the list and update the <poin-
ter>.

Variables as functions

To realize the local transition function it was assumed that in general the following code is acceptable to the LISP interpreter.
```
((LAMBDA (<var>)
    ...
    (<var> <arg1> <arg2> ...)
    ...
  <fn>)
```

The value of <var> gives the function name <fn>. There are some LISP dialects (e.g. INTERLISP) where - for good reasons - this is not allowed. Instead you have to write

```
((LAMBDA (<var>)
    ...
    (FUNCALL <var> <arg1> <arg2> ...)
    ...)
 <fn>)
```

APPENDIX B

The following listing gives the definition of those functions of the interpreter which are not given explicitly in the text. They are presented in alphabetical order.

```
(DEFMACRO-DISPLACE TRACER
     (VALUE INFO-VAR)
  '(TRACER ,(SELECTQ (ARCTYPE ARC)
              [SEND 'PUSH-TRACE?]
              'ARC-TRACE? )
          ,VALUE
          , @(EVAL INFO-VAR)))) )

(DEFMACRO CAT
     (CATEGORIES . ACTIONS)
  '(MAPC (F:L (ENTRY)
            (CATCH (AND
                   [MEMQ (CAR ENTRY
                        ,(COND
                            [(ATOM CATEGORIES)
                             ''(,CATEGORIES)]
                            [T '',CATEGORIES])]
                    [LETL (CSYNTAX [LIST * ENTRY])
                    [SETQ ** (GETF NF) *** ENTRY]
                    , @ACTIONS])
                  EVAL-ARC))
        (CDR CSYNTAX))) )

(DEFUN CLEAR-REGS EXPR
        (N STACK)
    (DO ((STACK STACK (CDR STACK))
```

```
              (HEAD NIL HEAD))
         ((NULL STACK) (NREVERSE HEAD))
         (COND
            [(GREATERP (CDAAR STACK) N)
             (RETURN (COND
                        [HEAD (NCONC (NREVERSE HEAD) STACK)]
                        [T STACK] ))]
            [(LESSP (CDAAR STACK) N)
             (PUSH HEAD (CAR STACK))]) ) )

(DEFMACRO EVAL-STATE
     (STATY)
   (SETQ STATY (EVAL STATY))
   (STATE-TRACER T MOVE-TO-INFO)
   (COND
      [(COMPILED-STATE? STATY)
       (LIST STATY)]
      [(ONEP (LENGTH (GETOUTARCS STATY)))
       '(CATCH (EVAL-ARC ',(CAR (GETOUTARCS STATY)))
             ,STATY)]
      [T '(CATCH (MAPC (F:L (ARC)
                         (CATCH (EVAL-ARC ARC)
                             EVAL-ARC))
                      ',(GETOUTARCS STATY))
                    ,STATY)]) ) )

(DEFUN EVALN MACRO
         (L)
   (CONS 'PROGN
         (EVAL (CADR L))) )

(DEFUN GETF FEXPR
          (ARGL)
   (LETL (FEATURE (CAR ARGL))
      (DO ((L (CDADR CSYNTAX) (CDDR L)))
         ((OR
            [EQ (CAR L) FEATURE]
            [NULL L] )
          (CADR L)))) )

(DEFUN GROUP FEXPR
         (ARCS)
   (MAPC (F:L (ARC)
```

```
                    (CATCH (EVAL-ARC ARC) EVAL-ARC)
                    (AND
                      BACKTRACE
                      [THROW NIL EVAL-ARC]))
              ARCS) )

(DEFMACRO JUMP
        (STATE . ACTIONS)
     '(PROGN (SETQ ** (GETF NF))
             ,@ACTIONS
             (TO1 ,(KWOTE-ATOM STATE)
                  T))) )

(DEFUN KWOTE-ATOM EXPR
            (X)
       (COND
         [(OR
            [NULL X]
            [NUMBERP X]
            [NOT
              [ATOM X] ]) X]
         [T (LIST 'QUOTE X)]) )

(DEFMACRO LOOKAHEADW
        (WORDS)
       (COND
         [(NOT
            [NON-CONSUMING-ARC? ARC])
          '(PROGN (AND
                    [EQ (CURR-SYNTAX INPUTBUFFER) (
                     CURR-SYNTAX SYNTAX)]
                    [READ-IN])
                  (MEMQ (CADDR SYNTAX)
                        ',WORDS))]
         [T '(MEMQ *
                 ',WORDS)]) ) )

(DEFUN MEMBC EXPR
          (CATEGORY LEXLIST)
       (AND
         [ATOM CATEGORY]
         [SETQ CATEGORY (CONS CATEGORY)])
```

```
    (DO ((LI LEXLIST (CDR LI)))
        ((OR
          [NULL LI]
          [MEMQ (CAAR LI) CATEGORY])
         LI)) )

(DEFUN PARSE1 EXPR
           (MACHINE)
    (LETL (INPUTBUFFER (INPUT-BUFFER MACHINE)
           OUTPUTBUFFER (OUTPUT-BUFFER MACHINE))
        (INIT-READ-IN)
        (LETL (STATE MACHINE
               POP-STACK (LIST (LIST (CONS T NIL)))
               SYNTAX (COPY-BUFFER INPUTBUFFER)
               CSYNTAX (CURR-SYNTAX INPUTBUFFER)
               ATN-CL 1
               REG-STACK NIL
               * (CURR-WORD INPUTBUFFER)
               ** NIL
               VALUE NIL
               PARSELIST NIL
               BACKTRACE NIL)
            ((LAMBDA (TO1 START-TIME)
                (SETQ VALUE
                     (CATCH (CATCH (TO1 STATE T) (EVAL-ARC)
                            TOP-LEVEL))
                (MSG T
                   "parsing time: "
                   (- (TIME) START-TIME)))
             (GET 'TO1 'TOP-DOWN/DEPTH-FIRST)
             (TIME))
            (PRETTYS VALUE)
            (SELECTQ PARSENR
                [1 VALUE]
                PARSELIST )))  )

(DEFMACRO-DISPLACE REG-TRACER
      (VALUE INFO-VAR)
   '(TRACER REG-TRACE?
           ,VALUE
           ,@(EVAL INFO-VAR)) )
```

```
(DEFMACRO ROOT
     (ROOTS . ACTIONS)
   '(AND
     [MEMQ (SETQ ** (GETF NF))
          ,(COND
               [(ATOM ROOTS)
               ''(,ROOTS)]
               [T '',ROOTS] ) ]
     [PROGN ,@ACTIONS] ) )

(DEFMACRO SEEK
     (PHRASETYPE . ACTIONS)
   (LETL (SEP-ACTIONS (SEPARATE-SEEK-ACTIONS ACTIONS))
      '(PROGN , @(CAR SEP-ACTIONS)
              (CATCH (SEEK* ,(KWOTE-ATOM STATE)
                           (1+ ATN-CL)
                           (CONS (CONS ',(CADR
                                           SEP-ACTIONS)
                                       ',PHRASETYPE)
                                 POP-STACK))
             SEEK)))   )

(DEFMACRO SEEK*
     (STATE ATN-CL POP-STACK)
   (TRACER PUSH-TRACE? NIL (T %PUSH-INDENT) "pushing")
   '(LETL (POP-STACK ,POP-STACK
         ATN-CL ,ATN-CL)
      (TO1 ,STATE T)) )

(DEFMACO SEND
     (PHRASETYPES FORM . ACTIONS)
   '(AND
     [MEMQ ',(CADR (CAR POP-STACK))
          ',PHRASETYPES]
     [PROGN ,@ACTIONS
            (SEND* (CDR POP-STACK) (CAAR POP-STACK) ,FORM (
            1- ATN-CL) (CLEAR-REGS ATN-CL REG-STACK)] ) )

(DEFMACRO SEND*
     (POP-STACK ACTIONS * ATN-CL REG-STACK)
   '(LETL (REG-STACK ,REG-STACK
          POP-STACK ,POP-STACK
          * ,*
```

```
                    ATN-CL ,ATN-CL
                    ACTIONS ,ACTIONS)
              (AND
                [TERMINATED?]
                [TERMINATE-PARSE *] )
              (EVALN ACTIONS)) )

(DEFUN SENDR MACRO
          (ARGL)
    (CADR (LIST '>
                   (SETR-MACRO ARGL
                               NIL
                               '(1+ ATN-CL)))) )

(DEFUN SENDRQ MACRO
          (ARGL)
    (CADR (REPLACE ARGL
                    (LIST '>
                           (SETR-MACRO ARGL
                                       T
                                       (1+ 'ATN-CL))))) )

(DEFUN SEPARATE-SEEK-ACTIONS EXPR
          (L)
    (PROG (PRE POST)
         (MAPC [F:L  (X)
                   (SELECTQ (CAR X)
                       [SETQ X
                             (CADDR X)]
                       NIL )
                   (SELECTQ (CAR X)
                       [(SENDR SENDRQ)
                        (PUSH PRE X)]
                       [> (PUSH PRE (CADR X))]
                       (PUSH POST X) )]
               L)
         (RETURN (LIST (NREVERSE PRE) (NREVERSE POST)))) )

(DEFUN SETR MACRO
          (ARGL)
    (SETR-MACRO ARGL NIL 'ATN-CL) )

(DEFUN SETR-MACRO EXPR
          (ARGL Q? LEVEL)
```

```
   (POP ARGL)
   (DO ((REGS ARGL (CDDR REGS))
        (REGISTER (CAR ARGL) (CADDR REGS))
        (VALUE (CADR ARGL) (CADDDR REGS))
        (CODE NIL CODE))
       ((NULL REGS)
        (COND
           [(NULL (CDR CODE))
            (CAR CODE)]
           [T (CONS 'PROGN (NREVERSE CODE))] ) )
       (AND
         Q?
         [SETQ VALUE (KWOTE VALUE)])
       (REG-TRACER (PUSH CODE
                         '(**SETR** ',REGISTER
                                    ,LEVEL
                                    ,VALUE))
                   SET-REG-INFO)) )

(DEFUN SETRQ MACRO
         (ARGL)
   (DISPLACE ARGL
            (SETR-MACRO ARGL T 'ATN-CL)) )

(DEFMACRO STATE-TRACER
      (VALUE INFO-VAR)
   \(TRACER STATE-TRACE? ,VALUE ,(EVAL INFO-VAR)) )

(DEFUN SWITCHOFF EXPR
         (%SWITCH)
   (AND
     [EVAL %SWITCH]
     [SET %SWITCH NIL] ) )

(DEFUN SWITCHON EXPR
         (%SWITCH %VALUE)
   (SET %SWITCH %VALUE) )

(DEFUN TERMINATE-PARSE EXPR
         (*)
   (MSG T "SUCCESSFUL PARSE.")
   (COND
     [(EQ PARSENR 'ALL)
```

```
        (PUSH PARSELIST *)
       NIL]
      [(ONEP PARSENR)
       (COND
          [(NULL PARSELIST)
           (THROW * TOP-LEVEL)]
          [T (PUSH PARSELIST *)
             (THROW PARSELIST TOP-LEVEL)] ) ]
      [(NUMBERP PARSENR)
       (SETQ PARSENR (1- PARSENR))
       (PUSH PARSELIST *)
       NIL]
      [T (ERROR (MSG -1 PARSENR T "BAD PARSENR"))] )   )

(DEFUN TERMINATED? EXPR
         NIL
   (NULL POP-STACK) )

(DEFMACRO-DISPLACE TO
      (STATE)
  '(TO1 ,(KWOTE-ATOM STATE)
        ,(NON-CONSUMING-ARC? ARC)))) )

(DEFPROP TO1
 (LAMBDA (STATE NOMOVEFLAG)
     (COND
        [NOMOVEFLAG (NCONC NEWACFS
                       (LIST (LIST STATE SYNTAX CSYNTAX *
                          ** REG-STACK POP-STACK)))]
        [T (NCONC NEWACFS
                (LIST (LIST STATE (CDR SYNTAX) (CADR SYNTAX)
                       (CAADR SYNTAX) (GETF NF) REG-STACK
                      POP-STACK))] )
     NIL)
 TOP-DOWN/BREADTH-FIRST)

(DEFPROP TO1
 (LAMBDA (STATE NOMOVEFLAG)
     (COND
        [NOMOVEFLAG (SETQ * (CAR CSYNTAX))
                    (EVAL-STATE STATE)]
        [T (LETL (SYNTAX (CDR SYNTAX)
                   CSYNTAX (CADR SYNTAX)
```

```
                    * (CAADR SYNTAX)
                    ** (GETF (CAADR SYNTAX)))
                 (EVAL-STATE STATE))] )
      (SETQ BACKTRACE T)
      (STATE-TRACER NIL FAILING-FROM-INFO))
 TOP-DOWN/DEPTH-FIRST)

(DEFMACRO TRACER
      (TR-FLAG TR-VALUE . TR-MESSAGES)
    'PROG2 (AND
            ,TR-FLAG
            [MSG ,@TR-MESSAGES] )
          ,TR-VALUE) )

(DEFUN TRYPAR FEXPR
          (ARGL)
   ((LAMBDA (TO1)
       (DO ((ACFS (LETL (NEWACFS '(NIL))
                     (MAPC (F:L (ARC)
                             (CATCH (EVAL-ARC ARC)
                              EVAL-ARC))
                        ARGL)
                     (DELQ NIL NEWACFS))
                 (MAPCAN [F:L (ACF)
                          ((LAMBDA (STATE SYNTAX CSYNTAX
                                     * ** REG-STACK
                                    POP-STACK)
                             (LETL (NEWACFS '(NIL))
                               (EVAL-STATE STATE)
                               (DELQ NIL NEWACFS)))
                           (CAR ACF)
                           (CADR ACF)
                           (CADDR ACF)
                           (CADDDR ACF)
                           (CAR (CDDDDR ACF))
                           (CADR (CDDDDR ACF))
                           (CADDR (CDDDDR ACF)))]
                    (DELQ T ACFS)))))
            ((NULL ACFS) (THROW NIL EVAL-ARC))))
     (GET 'TO1 'TOP-DOWN/BREADTH-FIRST)) )
```

```
(DEFUN TRYSEQ FEXPR
          (ARGL)
   (LABELS ((TO1 (GET 'TO1 'TOP-DOWN/DEPTH-FIRST)))
           (MAPC (F:L (ARC)
                      (CATCH (EVAL-ARC ARC) EVAL-ARC))
                 ARGL)) )

(DEFMACRO TST
      (LABEL . ACTIONS)
    '(AND
      [,LABEL '(,CSYNTAX)]
      [PROGN ,@ACTIONS] )) )

(DEFMACRO VERIFY
      (TEST DEST)
    (AND
     [STATEP DEST]
     [PUTPROP DEST STATE 'DIRECTED-BACKUP])
    (OR
     DEST
     [SETQQ DEST EVAL-ARC])
    '(OR
      ,TEST
      [THROW (VERIFY-TRACER ',DEST)
             ,DEST] ) )

(DEFUN VERIFY-TRACER EXPR
          (DEST)
    (SELECTQ DEST
         [EVAL-ARC (TRACER ARC-TRACE? NIL (T %ARC-INDENT)
                      "failing from arc.")]
         [TOP-LEVEL (TRACER TRACE? NIL "GIVING UP COMPLETELY.")]
         [SEEK (TRACER PUSH-TRACE? NIL
               "GIVING UP THIS SUBNET.")]
         (TRACER STATE-TRACE? NIL (T %STATE-INDENT)
         "FAILING BACK TO" DEST ".") ) )

(DEFMACRO WORD
      (WORDS . ACTIONS)
    '(AND
      [MEMQ *
            ,(COND
```

```
        [ (ATOM WORDS)
          '' (,WORDS) ]
          [T '',WORDS] ) ]
    [PROGN (SETQ ** (GETF NF))
         ,@ACTIONS] ) )
```

(NIL)

REFERENCES

Allen, J., Anatomy of LISP, McGraw Hill, [1978]

Bates, M., "The Theory and Practice of Augmented Transition Network Grammars", in Bolc, L. (ed.), Natural Language Communication with Computers, [1978]

Bolc, L., (ed.), "Natural Language Communication with Computers", Lecture Notes in Computer Science, vol. 63, Springer-Verlag, New York, Berlin, Heidelberg, [1978]

Burton, R.R., Woods, W.A., "A Compiling System for Augmented Transition Networks", Preprints of 6. COLING, University of Ottawa, Ottawa, [1976]

Charniak, E., McDermott, D., Riesbeck, C., "Artificial Intelligence Programming", Lawrence Erlbaum,[1980]

Christaller, T., Metzing, D. (eds.), ATN-Grammatiken, Band 1-2, Einhorn-Verlag, Berlin, [1979]

Christaller, T., Metzing, D., "Parsing Interactions and a Multi-Level Parser Formalism based on Cascaded ATNs", in Sparck Jones, Wilks (eds.), Automatic Natural Language Parsing, CSCM-10, Cognitive Science Centre, University of Essex, Colchester, [1982]

-, Di Primio, F., "A Poor Man's Flavor System" (to appear)

Finin, T.W. "An Interpreter and Compiler for Augmented Transition Networks. University of Illinois, Coordinated Science Lab. Report T-48, Urbana, [1977]

Hadden, G.D., NETEDI: An Augmented Transition Network Editor, Coordina-
    ted Science Lab. Report T-48, Urbana, University of Illinois
    [1977]

Hewitt, C., "Viewing Control Structures as Patterns of Passing Messages",
    Artificial Intelligence, Vol. 8, pp. 323-364

Jameson, T., "Ein Compiler für einen rekursiven ATN-Interpreter", in
    Petöfi, Metzing (eds.), Jährlicher Bericht zum Projekt Textver-
    arbeitung, Bielefeld [1980]

Kaplan, R.M., "A General Syntactic Processor", in Rustin (ed.), Natural
    Language Processing. [1973]

Kay, A., Goldberg, A., SMALLTALK-72 User's Manual. Xerox, Palo Alto,
    [1972]

Kerp, A., "ATN's: Considerations about a new Formalism, a Parallel In-
    terpreter, and other application areas", (in German) in
    Christaller, Metzing ATN Grammatiken II, [1980], pp. 127-147

Laubsch, J.H., et.al., MACLISP-manual. Institut für Informatik, Univer-
    sität Stuttgart,[1976]

Moon, D.A., MacLISP-Manual. MIT, Project MAC, Cambridge, MA, [1974]

Moses, J., The Function of FUNCTION in LISP. AI Memo, MIT, [1970]

Pereira, F.C.N., Warren, D.H.D., "Definite Clause Grammars for Language
    Analysis - a Survey of the Formalism and a Comparison with
    ATNs", in Artificial Intelligence, vol. 13, [1980], 231-278

Quillian, R., "Semantic Memory", in Minsky (ed.), Semantic Information
    Processing, MIT Press, [1968]

Raulefs, P., Fischer, H.L., "Design Rationale for the Interactive Pro-
    gramming Language CSSA for Asynchronous Multiprocessor Systems",
    Comp. Science Dept., Univ. Bonn, [1979]

Reynolds, J.C., "Definitional Interpreters for Higher Order Programming
    Languages", Proceedings of the ACM Conference, [1972]

Rustin, R. (ed.), "Natural Language Processing", Algorithmic Press,
    New York, [1973]

Steele, G., RABBIT: A Compiler for SCHEME, MIT, Cambridge, MA, [1978]

Teitelman, W., INTERLISP-Manual, Xerox, Palo Alto, [1978]

Weinreb, D., Moon, D., Lisp Machine Manual, MIT, Cambridge, MA [1979]

Winston, P.H., Artificial Intelligence, Addison-Wesley, [1978]

- , Horn, LISP, Addison-Wesley, [1981]

Woods, W.A., "Transition Network Grammars for Natural Language Analysis",
        CACM, 13, pp. 591-606, [1970]

- , Research in Natural Language Understanding, BBN, Report No. 3963
        [1978]

- , "Cascaded ATN Grammars", Journal of ACL, vol. 6, [1980], pp. 1-18

Abbreviations

ACL   Association of Computing Linguistics
ACM   Association of Computing Machinery
BBN   Bolt Beranek and Newman, Inc.
CACM   Communications of ACM
COLING   International Conference on Computational Linguistics
IJCAI   International Joint Conference on Artificial Intelligence
MIT   Massachusetts Institute of Technology

Compiling Augmented Transition Networks into MacLisp

Joachim Laubsch[1] and Karl Barth[2]

CONTENTS

[1] The Open University Milton Keynes, England

[2] Institut für Informatik, Universität Stuttgart, FRG

1. INTRODUCTION

It has been demonstrated in a wide variety of "question answering systems" and other natural language interfaces that ATN-grammars provide a practical tool which can accommodate a variety of language theories. We report here on the experience we gathered at the "Man Machine Communication Group" (University of Stuttgart) with the compilation of Augmented Transition Networks into Lisp, and some applications of ATN-grammars.

The parsing component in our projects consists of an ATN-MacLisp Compiler [Barth, 1978], a version of Burton's ATN-InterLisp Compiler [Burton & Woods, 1976], adapted to run under MacLisp for the TR44Ø Computer [Laubsch, 1976]. ATN-grammars were written in our group for various microworlds in order to study the utility of semantic grammars [Rathke et. al., 1979] and frame-based parsing [Laubsch, 1979; Laubsch & Roesner, 198Ø].

Since many of the issues dealing with an efficient execution of ATN-code are very specific to our computing environment, and therefore of little interest to the outside reader, we will explain the general and transferable ideas involved in compiling ATN-grammars, but go into sufficient detail to enable the reader to understand and modify a given compiler, or write a compiler along those lines. The issue of understanding a compiler may actually be quite valuable for the computational linguist who wants to test out an idea which needs a slight extension of the ATN formalism.

We must ignore here the important problem of a comfortable user-interface that supports interactive grammar development and testing. Such a system could be based upon the philosophy of InterLisp's DWIM [Teitelman, 1972], and developed into a "linguistic laboratory" in which people can freely experiment with language theories and models of human verbal communication. The advantage of embedding the ATN-language in a Lisp environment results mainly from the ease of adapting interactive monitoring devices (Steppers, Trace and Break), as well as advanced documentation and editing facilities (like Emacs and Info [Stallman, 1979]) into the embedded language. Unfortunately, a perfect development system does not exist yet. The complexity of such a linguistic laboratory, as well as the high computational demand for good development and debugging tools, make it necessary to have a powerful personal computer (such as the MIT Lisp machine [Bawden et. al., 1979] to provide an environment that would mean a step in leaping over Winograd's famous "complexity barrier".

2. APPROACHES TO ATN-COMPILATION

The syntax and semantics of Augmented Transition Networks are explained in [Bobrow & Fraser, 1969, Woods, 1970, and Bates, 1978]. A simple ATN-compiler (without back-tracking) is described by [Winston & Horn, 1981], and an ATN-interpreter can be found in [Charniak et. al., 1980] or [Christaller, 1980].

The goal of compiling ATNs is to speed up execution. The price to be paid is less debugging information. In this sense, ATN-programming is like Lisp programming in an interpreter/compiler environment: Only after you are confident that a function behaves as intended, you compile it and will then be unable to step it or break into it without reloading the interpreted definition.

We will outline two compilation techniques. The first, originally developed by Burton for InterLisp [Burton & Woods, 1976], compiles ATNs into a single low level parser-machine, and requires recompilation of the entire grammar after a change. The second technique compiles into relatively high-level language constructs, as they are available in MacLisp [Moon, 1978], or Lisp-Machine-Lisp [Weinreb & Moon, 1981], and relies on their powerful compiler to produce efficient run-time code.

Compilation into a low level parser machine has the advantage of transportability, which may be important for dedicated applications in "natural language front end" user interfaces. In many CAI-type situations, information retrieval, text processing, or electronic mail applications a simple natural language facility could be beneficial to the user, but there are only small computing resources available, insufficient to support a complex Lisp system (whose functionality may not be needed by the remaining applications).

Compilation of ATNs into a language with features such as recursion, backtracking and automatic garbage collection is much easier done (because much work can be left to the host language compiler), and also may lead to more efficient code, since the host language compiler can be optimized for the target machine to optimally deal with these higher level constructs. The second point in favor of this approach is that in Lisp typically an interpreter is available which may be used for run-time debugging and incremental program development. It then becomes unnecessary to have both an interpreter as well as a compiler for ATNs. Aside from the computation cost for a dual system, usually much effort must be spent in order for both interpreter and compiler to behave truly according to the same semantics.

3. COMPILATION INTO A PARSER MACHINE

In an ATN-interpreter, the ATN virtual machine runs compiled, but the actual evaluation of the ATN-grammar is done interpretatively. (It may be a timely project to design an ATN-chip, using the techniques developed for the SCHEME chip [Steele & Sussmann, 1979].) A compiler transforms the ATN-grammar into a program of some target language, thus removing a level of interpretation. The following features of ATNs have to be simulated in the target language:

* recursive control structure

* back-track control structure

* a tree-structured allocation of registers

[Burton, 1976] took the approach that the target language may be quite low level (e.g. like C or BCPL), and wrote a compiler that produces InterLisp code which could easily be transformed to such a language. We adapted this compiler [Barth, 1978] to run under MacLisp (TR440), and will explain the fundamental ideas of the ATN-MacLisp Compiler.

For the sake of clarity, we excluded the following ATN-features in this exposition. They will not pose any essentially new problems in the design of a compiler:

(1) A HOLD list as a place to keep structures which can be later consumed by VIR arcs.

(2) Alternative lexical interpretations and multiple word senses within a category.

(3) The "well formed substring table" to avoid reparsings.

Burton's compiler deals with all of these features and it is possible to selectively turn them off. The compiler produces for a given grammar as input a single function, called PARSER (see Fig. 1):

```
001    (defun PARSER (*cf-top*)
                    ; *cf-top* = active configuration frame
002      (prog (state stack node regs * *R*)
003        spread-acf
004              (unpack-array (Config-Stack *cf-top*)
005                            state stack node regs)
006        evalarc  (branch state
007                         success detour np np-art np-quant
008                         np-adj np-adj-1 np-n np-n-1 np-n-push
009                         pp pp-prep pp-prep-push pp-np)
010        success  (and  (emptyp-node node) (return *))
011        detour   (cond (alts (setq *cf-top* (alts-first))
012                             (go spread-acf))
013                       (t (return (failure))))
                    ; <grammar specific code>
```

Fig. 1: Main Control Section of the Parser

PARSER's input is a data-structure consisting of the sentence to be parsed, the starting node of the grammar, an initial register assignment, and possibly a return stack. Its output is either a structure created by BUILDQ or a symbol that indicates failure. PARSER also side-effects a Push-Down-Stack of alternatives in such a way, that PARSER could be resumed after returning, i.e. if one wants to use it as a generator co-routine in conjunction with some other process.

PARSER consists of a large PROG that contains labels for each ATN node and further auxiliary labels for continuations. A continuation is a state of the ATN-machine which will be resumed after successfully processing the subATN PUSHed to.

Lines 1-13 constitute the main control section and will be the same for each compiled grammar (except the branch statement at lines 6-9). We will explain an example of grammar specific code below. The PROG variables (line 2) keep the state of the ATN-machine. A machine state is represented as a stack-frame on the configuration stack (Config-Stack) and identified by the variables state, stack, node and regs:

state: a label describing the ATN-node and the arc emanating from that node. It is the next choice to be tried.

node: the (remaining) sentence to be analysed. If the sentence is to be represented as a list, node is the tail of that list starting with the element pointed to by the scanner. A more advanced implementation would use a chart instead. PARSER would then have to allow for alternative edges.

stack: a machine state to be restored after a POP, which may be represented as a pointer to a configuration frame.

regs: an association list (or similar data structure) that binds register names to their values.

PARSER is called with an initial configuration frame and constructs a new frame for every choice that might have to be undone. The auxiliary variable * is used according to ATN semantics (.e.g. the current word or a structure returned by POP). The auxiliary variable *R* is a temporary variable.

In lines 4-5 (Fig. 1) the configuration frame is spread from the stack frame into the state variables. Here, UNPACK-ARRAY could be implemented as a macro that performs the expansion:

```
        (unpack-array (Config-Stack *cf-top*)
                state stack node regs)
    ==>
(SETQ STATE (CONFIG-STACK *CF-TOP*)
        STACK (CONFIG-STACK (+ *CF-TOP* 1))
        NODE (CONFIG-STACK (+ *CF-TOP* 2))
        REGS (CONFIG-STACK (+ *CF-TOP* 3)))
```

Then the branch statement at line 6 is executed. Depending on the value of state, control will be given to the code that deals with this particular state. BRANCH happened to be introduced as a SUBR into our MacLisp, but could have been defined as a macro that expands:

```
        (branch state
                success detour np ...)
    ==>
(CASEQ STATE
        (SUCCESS (GO SUCCESS))
        (DETOUR (GO DETOUR))
        (NP (GO NP))  ...
        (T (LOSE |Unseen branch tag: ~S| STATE)))
```

The states SUCCESS and DETOUR are special in that they are no ATN nodes. At SUCCESS (line 10) PARSER is exited, if there is no string left. (Instead of emptyp-node this may be a more general user-supplied predicate.) At DETOUR (line 11) back-tracking is handled: If alternatives have been

created by MK-ALTARC, the last alternative is taken off, and the machine
state is restored. If no alternative remains, PARSER is left with the
value of the failure function, which may be user-defined. Control is
passed to DETOUR if all arcs from a node have been tried (see lines 41,
50 and 61 in Fig. 3 below).

We will consider a simple NP network (given by [Bates, 1978])as an example to study the grammar specific code generated by the compiler. Fig.
2 shows the ATN-code that will be compiled:

```
001     (defATN np
002       (np      (cat art t
003                   (setr art (buildq ((art *))))
004                   (to np-art))
005               (jump np-art t))
006       (np-art  (cat quant t
007                   (setr quant (buildq ((quant *))))
008                   (to np-quant))
009               (jump np-quant t))
010       (np-quant (cat adj t
011                   (addr adjs (buildq (@ (adj)    (*))
012                                      (getf degree)))
013                   (to np-quant))
014               (jump np-adj t))
015       (np-adj (cat n t
016                   (setr n * nu (getf number))
017                   (to np-n))
018                (cat n t
019                   (addl adjs (buildq (adj (np (n *) (nu  )))
020                                       (getf number)))
021                   (to np-adj)))
022       (np-n (push pp (ppstart)
023                   (addl nmods *)
024                   (to np-n))
025               (pop (buildq (@ (np) + + + ((n +)) ((nu +)) +)
026                       art quant adjs n nu nmods
027                   (detagree))))
028
029     (defATN pp
030       (pp      (cat prep t
031                   (setr prep *)
```

```
Ø32                     (to pp-prep)))
Ø33       (pp-prep (push np (npstart)
Ø34                     (setr np *)
Ø35                     (to pp-np)))
Ø36       (pp-np    (pop (buildq (pp (prep +) +) prep np) t)))
```

Fig. 2: ATN-Code for a Noun Phrase

In Fig. 2 defATN is the defining function for a subATN. It is a macro
that could call an incremental compiler. The nodes are all local and
are prefixed with the subATN-name. An editor such as EMACS [Stallman,
1979] can be used to quickly find any subATN and node within it through
the use of the TAGS feature (an automatic indexing of symbolic names
with locations in a set of files).
Compilation procedes in two stages:

(1) From the ATN-grammar, Lisp code is generated by the ATN-
    compiler and inserted into the parser function.

(2) PARSER is compiled by the Lisp compiler into a SUBR.

Fig. 3 shows the grammar specific code, as the compiler generates it
for the noun phrase ATN of Fig. 2.

Each ATN-arc is translated into a COND statement. The predicate is arc
specific: in line 14 of Fig. 3 (which corresponds to line 2 of Fig. 2),
the ArCAT predicate tests, whether * is an article. If a test where
given, it would be wrapped into an AND with the ArCAT. The predicate
ArCAT could have been defined as:

```
(defmacro ArCAT (cat)
   '(setq *R* (get (car node) ',cat)))
```

The MacLisp function DEFMACRO is a macro definer. The variables in the
lambda-list are bound unevaluated to the arguments, and the body is
evaluated. This constructs a form which will be evaluated instead of
the original macro-call. The back-quote notation reverses Lisp's quo-
ting convention: within a "`"-form, only elements preceded by a ","
are evaluated and elements preceded by ",@" are evaluated and spliced
into the list (as append would do).

```
014     np          (cond ((ArCAT art)
015                        (mk-altarc np-art)
016                        (setr art `((art , *)))
017                        (doto np-art)
018                        (go np-art)))
019     np-art      (cond ((ArCAT quant)
020                        (mk-altarc np-quant)
021                        (setr quant `((quant , *)))
022                        (doto np-quant)
023                        (go np-quant)))
024     np-quant    (cond ((ArCAT adj)
025                        (mk-altarc np-adj)
026                        (addr adjs
027                             `(adj , @(getfcat degree) , *))
028                        (doto np-quant)
029                        (go np-quant)))
030     np-adj      (cond ((ArCAT n)
031                        (mk-altarc np-adj-1)
032                        (setr n * nu (getfcat number))
033                        (doto np-n)
034                        (go np-n)))
035     np-adj-1    (cond ((ArCAT n)
036                        (addl adjs
037                             `(adj (np (n , *)
038                                        (nu ,(getfcat number )))))
039                        (doto np-adj)
040                        (go np-adj))
041                        (t (go detour)))
042     np-n        (cond ((ppstart)
043                        (mk-altarc np-n-1)
044                        (dopush pp np-n-push)
045                        (go pp)))
046     np-n-1      (cond ((detagree)
047                        (dopop `(np ,@ :art ,@ :quant ,@ :adjs
048                                 (n , :N) (NU , :NU) ., :nmods))
049                        (go evalarc))
050                        (t (go detour)))
051     np-n-push   (add1 nmods *)
052                 (go np-n)
053     pp          (cond ((ArCAT prep)
054                        (setr prep *)
```

```
055                         (doto pp-prep)
056                         (go pp-prep))
057                         (t (go detour)))
058     pp-prep     (cond ((npstart)
059                         (dopush np pp-prep-push)
060                         (go np))
061                         (t (go detour)))
062     pp-prep-push
063             (setr np *)
064             (dopto pp-np)
065     pp-np       (dopop `(pp (prep , :prep) , :np))
066             (go evalarc)))
```

Fig. 3: Grammar Specific code of PARSER

Thus, (ArCAT adj) is the same as if we had written:

```
(setq *R* (get (car node) 'adj)).
```

ArCAT assumes that the lexical entry for the word is on its property
list, and side-effects *R* to the lexical information for this category.
All BUILDQ forms are similarly translated into the corresponding backquote forms.

Since also a JUMP arc springs from np (line 5 of Fig. 2), an alternative configuration frame has to be saved in case of a later back-up.
This is achieved by (mk-altarc np-art) (line 15, Fig. 3). The argument
of mk-altarc is the next arc to be taken. Since in this case it is an
unconditional JUMP arc, no interim label had to be created, but the destination of the JUMP could be taken. The situation is different at np-
adj (line 31, Fig. 3) where the next arc from np-adj is no JUMP arc.
Here, the label np-adj-1 is created and passed as the losing state to
mk-altarc. For the last arc from a node (e.g. the second CAT arc of np-
adj; line 18 of Fig. 2), no alternative has to be created (see line 35),
and if the arc-test fails, a back-up is initiated by passing control to
DETOUR (see line 41).

MK-ALTARC pushes a pointer to a configuration frame with the next arc
to be tried as the state onto a list of alternatives (alts). It could
have been defined as:

```
(defmacro mk-altarc (lose)
        `(push (save-config ',lose stack node regs) alts))
```

where SAVE-CONFIG creates a configuration frame and returns the pointer to it (i.e. an index to Config-Stack).

After saving the next arc, the action is performed. In our example grammar this consists only of various register operations (setR, setRQ, addR, addL). If there are several on a given arc (as in line 16 of Fig. 2), they will be collected into one large setR form (line 32 of Fig. 3). Note that * is translated to * which expands to a function that retrieves the root of the current lexical entry.

After the actions, the (TO <next-state>) form is compiled. In CAT, WRD, and MEM arcs this is accomplished by a DOTO and a go to <next-state> (see lines 17-18, etc.). DOTO moves the scanner to the next word (or next node of a chart) and updates the state to <next-state>. DOTO could have been defined as:

```
(defmacro doto (state)
        `(setq node (next-node node) state ',state))
```

(where next-node is cdr if the sentence were represented as a list of words.)

PUSH and POP arcs are a little more complicated. Aside from the alternative arc, a post-push label has to be created which is handed to the called subATN (e.g. at np-n the post-push label is np-n-push; see lines 44). This label serves as the machine state to be resumed after successful completion of a subnet. DOPUSH saves the configuration frame with the post-push label as state, the current stack, and regs. It then changes the state to the subATN, and if there were any SENDR pre-actions, they would have to be computed and transmitted as the value of regs. DOPUSH could have been defined as:

```
(defmacro dopush (subnet win & rest sendr)
        `(setq stack (save-config ',win stack node regs)
              regs  ,(and sendr (xsendr sendr))
              state ,subnet))
```

In MacLisp, the keyword & rest in a lambda-list means that trailing arguments will be bound to the lambda variable that follows & rest. Here sendr will be bound to the list of SENDR forms if there were any, Nil otherwise. XSENDR expands this SENDR form. After the return from the subnet, DOPTO changes the state to <next-state> (line 64 of Fig. 3).

A POP arc is translated into a DOPOP and GO to the label EVALARC. It

computes the result in the current environment, sets the machine state
to stack, and restores from it the variables state, stack, and regs.
Since indirect GO's are not allowed in compiled MacLISP, transfer is
made to the branch statement at EVALARC.
DOPOP could have been defined as:

```
(defmacro dopop (result)
         `(setq * ,result
               *cf-top* stack
               state (config-stack *cf-top*)
               stack (config-stack (1+ *cf-top*))
               regs  (config-stack (+ 3 *cf-top*)))))
```

As the previous macro definitions show, the final code of the parser
consists entirely of assignments, jumps, and primitive selectors and
constructors. In fact, it looks rather "unLispy", rather like code for
a register machine. The advantage of such code is that it can be transformed easily to a low level language.

The runtime package must also contain the storage management of the configuration stack and the list of alternatives (alts), as well as an interface to the lexicon. Registers are allocated in heap storage which
is automatically garbage collected in Lisp, and it is necessary to provide some mechanism for allocating them in a non-Lisp language (e.g. a
reference counting record allocation). If the configuration stack and
alts are kept after returning from PARSER, it is possible to use it as
a coroutine which can be resumed later on with another alternative. The
intervening computation (between leaving PARSER and resuming it) is not
nested in PARSER.

A drawback of this code is, that the grammar has to be compiled by the
Lisp compiler as a whole if changes at the ATN-level occurred. This
would make incremental ATN-programming with both stages of the compiler
impossible. Of course, one could run PARSER as an interpreted function
and patch changes into it. But this would make the entire grammar slow.
(A typical speed-up obtained by the MacLisp compiler is a factor of 12
for the SUBR version of PARSER against the EXPR version.) Also, the
monolithic PROG makes it impossible to successively AUTOLOAD portions
of the grammar. (AUTOLOAD is a MacLisp feature which allows automatic
loading of program libraries at run-time, when they are needed.)

Another undesirable feature is that the branch at evalarc becomes more
time consuming as the grammar grows. In fact, the most time-critical
functions of PARSER are branch and configuration saving and restoring.

(We found a factor of 5 improvement in speed after introducing hand-coded SUBRs for these.) Environment saving and restoring is handled very well in Lisp through lambda-binding, and control is powerful and fast through function calls. Our second implementation will explore the possibility of using these features.

The main advantage of this approach to compiling ATNs, transportability, is obtained by compiling the grammar on a powerful Lisp system, cross-compiling the generated code, and down-loading it to the target machine. In conjunction with an ATN-editor, the Lisp environment can serve as the development tool, while the target machine may be much less powerful.

4. A HIGH LEVEL INCREMENTAL COMPILER

The availability of a high performance compiler for MacLisp (on the DEC-10 or DEC-20) or on the Lisp machine makes it reasonable to compile into a larger subset of Lisp and still obtain efficient code. Recursion and back-track control are efficiently implemented in MacLisp itself and need not be simulated with low level constructs. Function calls are inherintly not more costly than gotos if appropriate optimization techniques are used by the Lisp compiler [Steele, 1977].

How can the arc transitions be translated into function calls? The idea is, to translate each node into a separate Lisp function, passing all the necessary state information along. This would eliminate the branch statement at evalarc and have the additional benefit that nodes can be incrementally compiled. Then the user may change any node of the ATN with an appropriate editor which realizes that a change has been made and redefines that function. (DefATN could be designed to do that.) MacLisp's function linkage mechanism would notice the redefinition and call the interpreted version of the redefined node. From time to time the user may ask the system to recompile all redefined ATN-nodes. This leads to three levels of ATN-code:

```
    (1)  ATN-language
                                      | ATN-Editor
                                      | + Compiler
    (2)  MacLisp interpreted functions    v
                                      | MacLisp
                                      | Compiler
    (3)  MacLisp compiled functions       v
```

Level 2 contains enough debugging information for meaningful Trace,
Break and Step packages. The ATN-compiler processes an ATN-node at a
time and implements the back-track information by the *catch and *throw
functions [Moon, 1978]. Briefly, *catch and *throw are special forms for
implementing non-local exits. An expression (*catch <tag> <form1>) is
evaluated as follows: first <tag> is evaluated as usual to produce the
tag of this catch. Then <form1> is evaluated and its value will be returned from the catch unless a throw with the same tag, (*throw <tag>
<form2>), is encountered in which case the value of <form2> is returned.

To enable the analysis of multiple parses (e.g. syntactic ambiguities),
the parser cannot be left, since after a throw the entire stack would
be unwound and all the information on it becomes inaccessible. (This
would not be so, if the stack-group mechanism of the Lisp machine were
used.) So, in order to use the parser as a generator (as can be con-
veniently done with PARSER), we have to pass a continuation function
down. That function will have control of whether or not to leave the
parser. It may, for example, accumulate all alternatives or do an arbitrary computation with some alternative and then request the next one.
To avoid clashes of free variables used in the continuation function
with those of the parser, a separate name space must be used for the
variables bound by the parser (while interpreted code is used).

```
001     (defun np (win lose node regs & aux (* (car node)) *R*)
002      (cond ((and (acat art)
003              (success?
004               (setq *R*
005                (*catch 'np
006                 (NP-ART win 'np (cdr node)
007                        (setr art `((art , *))))))))
008          *R*)
009         (t (NP-ART win lose node regs))))

010     (defun NP-ART (win lose node regs & aux (* (car node)) *R*)
011      (cond ((and (acat quant)
012              (success?
013               (setq *R*
014                (*catch 'NP-ART
015                 (NP-QUANT win 'NP-ART (cdr node)
016                        (setr quant `((quant , *))))))))
017          *R*)
018         (t (NP-QUANT win lose node regs))))
```

```
019    (defun NP-QUANT (win lose node regs & aux (* (car node)) *R*)
020     (cond ((and (acat adj)
021              (success?
022               (setq *R*
023                (*catch 'NP-QUANT
024                 (NP-QUANT win 'NP-QUANT (cdr node)
025                  (addr adjs
026                   `(adj ,@(getfcat degree) , *)))))))
027          *R*)
028         (t (NP-ADJ win lose node regs))))

029    (defun NP-ADJ (win lose node regs & aux (* (car node)) *R*)
030     (cond ((and (acat n)
031              (success?
032               (setq *R*
033                (*catch 'NP-ADJ
034                 (NP-N win 'NP-ADJ (cdr node)
035                  (setr n  * nu (getfcat number)))))))
036         *R*)
037        ((and (acat n)
038           (NP-ADJ win lose (cdr node)
039              (add1 adjs
040               `(adj (np (n , *)
041                  (nu ,(getfcat number ))))))))
042        (t (fail))))

043    (defun NP-N (win lose node regs & aux (* (car node)) *R*)
044     (cond ((and (ppstart)
045              (success?
046               (setq *R*
047                (*catch 'NP-N
048                 (&push PP 'NP-N NP-N np-n-push-pp)))))
049         *R*)
050        ((detagree)
051         (&pop `(np ,@ :art ,@ :quant ,@ :adjs
052              (n , :N) (NU , :NU) ., :nmods)))
053        (t (fail))))

054    (defun np-n-push-pp (* regs)  (addL nmods *))
055    (defun PP (win lose node regs & aux (* (car node)) *R*)
056     (cond ((acat prep)
057         (PP-PREP win lose (cdr node) (setr prep *)))
058        (t (fail))))
```

```
Ø59    (defun PP-PREP (win lose node regs & aux (* (car node)) *R*)
Ø6Ø    (cond ((npstart)
Ø61          (&push NP lose pp-np &setR-NP))
Ø62          (t (fail))))

Ø63    (defun PP-NP (win lose node regs & aux (* (car node)) *R*)
Ø64    (&pop `(pp (prep , :prep) , :np)))
```

Fig. 4: The Compiled Noun Phrase Grammar

We will examine the code produced for the noun phrase ATN of Fig. 2 to
illustrate the main points. Each node is compiled into a function with
the same name. The arguments of this function are:

win: a continuation to be used in case of success. It is
        implemented as an EXTEND datatype with the following
        fields:

   to: the continuation function to be called by a
               POP, i.e. the <next-state> of the calling
               PUSH arc

   win: a link to the stacked win configuration

   reg-fn: a function to be applied to the result of
               a POP

   regs: a data structure holding the registers to
               be used while applying reg-fn

lose: the failure continuation, i.e. a tag in some *catch
        which corresponds to the point until which the stack
        has to be unwound in order to try the next alternative.

node: the remaining string to be parsed.

regs: a data structure holding the registers, such as an
        association list of registers.

Each arc is compiled into a function call. (This may actually not be so,
since we can open-code transitions to nodes which have only a single
arc pointing to it.) The function called is <next-state> of the terminal act of the arc. This function is wrapped into a *catch whose tag
is passed as the failure continuation (lose) to the called function.

The last arc from a node can be treated specially, since (being a case
of tail-recursion) it can be translated to a function call with the old
win and lose continuations, thus saving to build the catch frame. The
entire PP-net (lines 54 to 64) contains no catch frames, since all nodes

are linearly connected: if any of the connecting arcs fails, the entire
PP-net fails.

The function is called with regs as a single expression that evaluates
to the new association list after all register setting actions are performed. If this is done without side effect, lambda-binding can be used
to save and restore registers The actions (setR, setRQ, addR, addL) macro
expand to a composite CONS, if we use Lisp style association lists for
registers.

In case we would admit actions that perform side effects (other than
register setting) in an ATN-dialect, one could use the UNWIND-PROTECT
construct of MacLisp to undo the side effects caused by a failing arc.
UNWIND-PROTECT forces expressions to be evaluated if its dynamic scope
is left (either regularly or through a throw). To translate ATNs with
side-effecting actions (other than of the SETR type), the generated code
would have the following form:

```
(*catch <lose tag>
       (unwind-protect
        (progn (<side-effect-function> . <args>)
               (<arc-function> win <lose tag> <node> <regs>))
        (<undo-side-effect-function> . <args>)))
```

The compiler must know what the inverse functions of the side effect
producing functions are.

The function returns failure if no arc succeeded from this node using
the function FAIL (e.g. line 58 in Fig. 4). It is defined as a macro
that performs a throw to the tag passed in as lose:

```
(defmacro fail () '(*throw lose *fail*))
```

The predicate success? evaluates to Nil for a failure and the next arc,
i.e. COND clause, will be tried (lines 30-42 in Fig. 4).

CAT, MEM, and WRS arcs differ only by the predicate used in the COND
clause. The JUMP arc is a degenerate form of these with the predicate
being T and passing node through.

PUSH and POP are treated differently from these arcs. For a PUSH arc
(compare line 61 of Fig. 4) of the form

```
(PUSH <state> <test> <pre-action> <action> (TO <next-state>))
```

the function called is <state> and a new win configuration is made with

to:	<next-state>
win:	the current win
reg-fn:	a function computing <action>, with the POPped result
regs:	the current regs

The lose continuation is either the current back-up point (e.g. the catch tag NP-N in line 47 of Fig. 4) or in the tail recursive case the current lose continuation (e.g. line 61 in Fig. 4). If there are SENDRs, the <pre-action> is passed as the regs argument. The macro &push implements PUSH and could have been defined as:

```
(defmacro &push (subnet lose to reg-fn &rest sendr)
  `(,subnet (mk-win ',to win ',reg-fn regs)
            lose
            node
            ,(and sendr (xsendr sendr))))
```

An example for a reg-fn is the generated function NP-N-PUSH-PP (lines 48 and 54) which implements the <action> of the PUSH arc.

For simple register setting operations, standard functions can be reused, like &setR-NP (line 61 of Fig. 4), which is defined as:

```
(defun &setR-NP (* regs) (setR NP *))
```

A POP arc (POP <form> <test>) will be expanded to a funcall expression with the function to be called being the to-field of the current win configuration. The remaining arguments of the funcall are the winner field of the win configuration, the lose of the environment of POP (i.e. either a new catch tag or in the tail-recursive case the current lose), and the regs resulting from applying the reg-fn of the win configuration to the <form> of POP. POP is implemented by &pop (see lines 51 and 64 of Fig. 4) which could have been defined as:

```
(defmacro &pop (popform &rest back-up-tag)
          `(funcall (to-node win)
                    (win win)
                    ,(if back-up-tag (car back-up-tag)
                         'lose)
                    node
                    (funcall (reg-fn win) ,popform (regs win)))))
```

A funcall is a cheap operation if the called function is compiled which
is always the case in this approach.

The parser may be started with an initialization function like parse:

```
(defmacro parse (atn-node sentence)
  `(progn (and (turnedon verbose)
               (format t "~%Parsing: ~S" ',sentence))
          (or (success?
               (*catch 'parse
                       (,atn-node Iwin 'parse ',sentence Nil)))
              (report-result "FAILURE"))))
```

The call to the parser is the catch form which calls the subATN with an
initial configuration (Iwin), that could be set up as:

```
(setq Iwin
  (mk-win   'atn-top                        ;to: decides when to stop
            'report-result                  ;win: continuation
            '(lambda (result regs) result)  ;result passed to win
          Nil)))                            ;initial registers
```

Its to-field may be the name of a function which controls whether to
back-track to the next alternative, e.g. like atn-top:

```
(defun atn-top (win lose node result)
       (cond ((null node) (funcall win result))
             (t (fail))))
```

In this case, if the sentence is empty, the first alternative of the
parse is passed to the win continuation which simply prints it. It is
possible to define a continuation function that would perform some arbitrary computation and then request the next alternative by failing.
This function would then be reinvoked with the next result. If it were
desired to resume the current computation, a closure could be made of
it and assigned as the to-field of Iwin. This would enable the use of
the ATN essentially as a generator.

It is possible to make certain optimizations. One of these is the loop
optimization for nodes which have arcs pointing to itself. Suppose the
node has the form:

```
(<node-1>  (CAT <category-1> <test-1> <action-1>
               (TO <node-1>))
           (CAT <category-2> <test-2> <action-2>
               (TO <node-x>)))
```

The first arc loops. It can be translated into an iteration (thus saving to build the catch frame and continuation) under certain conditions. (For simplicity we consider only the case with one looping and one non-looping arc, but the extension is straightforward.) If <category-1> and <category-2> are distinct, only one arc can succeed, and it is possible to reorder the arcs so that the looping one is treated first and transformed into an iteration. Even if <category-1> and <category-2> were not distinct, and it is possible to show that (not (and <test-1> <test-2>)) is true for any environment, then this optimization can be made.

Although we have not done so, it would be interesting to apply theorem proving techniques as developed by Boyer & Moore (1979) or Weyrauch (1977) to show that such a simplification can be made for arbitrary functions (e.g. like ppstart or detagree).

The incremental compiler produces somewhat more compact code which runs at about the same speed as PARSER. (There are many possibilities of achieving space-time trade-offs, and statistics will depend very much on the size and kind of grammar.) A disadvantage of the incremental compiler is the inconvenience of using it as a coroutine: any throw to the top-level (because of an error in one of the functions called by the continuation) would lose the alternative parses, while PARSER can keep its configuration stack as long as desired.

An implementation of an ATN-compiler which combines the good features of both would use stack-groups [Weinreb & Moon, 1981] or Interlisp's spaghetti stack [Bobrow & Wegbreit, 1973]. A stack-group contains binding information (like a closure) and control information (i.e. it remembers who called it, and where to resume). The code for the incremental compiler would not have to change very much, because stack groups can be used as functions: instead of leaving the win continuation with some result, a stack-group-return is performed. The entire stack-group is saved away, but can be resumed anytime later simply by calling it like a function. (See the Lisp Machine Manual for details.) It would be easy to implement cascaded ATNs as a set of coroutines, where each ATN corresponds to a single stack-group. Other applications like "island parsing" could be handled similarly with stack-groups.

5. SOME NATURAL LANGUAGE APPLICATIONS

Our first application of an ATN-Compiler was in a tutorial program on
Lisp [Lispler, Barth, 1977]. Its knowledge base is implemented as a semantic net, and contains information about Lisp's standard functions,
examples and important programming concepts. The student engages in a
mixed-initiative dialogue (in German), where he can request information
about some topic, or test examples which he is supposed to solve. The
student's query is translated into an expression which accesses the semantic network (semantic form). The information found there is printed
out to the student using a standard set of output templates. Here are
some examples:

```
>> Can you give me an example for a Cons?
semantic form: (FIND (IS-EXAMPLE-OF CONS))
>> How do I get the first element of it?
semantic form: (FIND (IS-FIRST-OF *LAST-REFERENCE*))
>> Which functions iterate on lists?
semantic form: (FIND (IS-FUNCTION-OF LISP)
                     (TYPE LIST-ITERATOR))
```

The parsing produces a syntactic tree which is transformed by a set of
production rules into a semantic form. The dialogue was often blocked
by missing lexical entries. An interactive vocabulary learning module
could be entered which queried the user about syntactic and semantic
features of the unknown word.

Another project used the CLOWN's microworld [Simmons & Bennet Novak,
1975] to generate simple animated line drawings, e.g.

```
>> The clown sailed with Fred from the pier to the beacon
```
would produce a sequence of snapshots portraying the event sequence.
The purpose of this study was to use semantic information at early stages during the syntactic analysis to disambiguate alternate parses.
Each time, a syntactic constituent (such as a PP) was found, its referent was computed. If no referent could be determined, back-up was sig-
nalled.

To explore the utility of a semantic grammar, a question-answering system about football was implemented [Rathke et. al., 1979]. A semantic
grammar similar in style to the one for SOPHIE [Brown et. al., 1974]
was written to produce expressions in a predicate calculus like language
(similar to MRL, see Woods, 1977), e.g. the for the query:

>> Tell me what club the mid field player Hansi Mueller plays for would directly produce the MRL expression:

```
(for the p1 person
      ((Nachname p1 'mueller)
       (Vorname p1 'Hansi)
       (Spiel-Funktion p1 'midfieldplayer))
      (for the v1 club
           ((Plays-for p1 v1)) (Printout v1)))
```

The resulting system demonstrated (as SOPHIE and HWIM did [Brown et.al. 1974] [Woods et. al., 1977]), that (1) query interpretation could be handled efficiently enough to be useful in real world applications, (2) the grammar to be constructed became quite large and almost entirely specific to the domain. The efficiency is due to semantic categories in CAT arcs which lead to subnets specific to this semantic category (thus avoiding back-up) and the direct construction of semantic forms in the ATN. We developed some guide lines and programming conventions that make it easier to construct grammars for new domains [Laubsch 1980]. If confronted with a new domain, we first identify domain-specific primitive acts (much like Schank's conceptual dependency theory [Schank, 1975]), the objects they refer to, the relations among these objects and rules for composition of acts. On the basis of this domain specific knowledge categorization, ATNs are written for each specific semantic category.

Frame-based parsing has the advantage of integrating semantic aspects, but leaving them out of the ATN-grammar. An interface of a semantic net with the ATN [Laubsch, 1979] serves to give certain subATNs a preferred activation state. If a case frame for example suggests that a case-slot should be a location, the PUSH to a noun phrase net for location would be preferred at a node which has several PUSH arcs. This way "safe PUSHes" are performed because they are syntactically as well as semantically expected. The compilation of PUSH arcs had to be changed, since the order of proceding through the arcs from a node is now dynamic.

6. CONCLUSIONS

ATNs make programming of grammars easier, without sacrificing efficiency in runtime execution, if appropriate compiling techniques are chosen. The universal nature of the ATN-language lends itself well to explore issues of semantic grammars and frame-driven parsing. Using ATNs does not commit one to a particular theory of language understanding.

Extensions to the ATN-language must be possible in order to be able to experiment with new control concepts or different input structures (e.g. the chart). In this situation, the availability of an ATN-interpreter or compiler as a "glass box" which can be inspected, understood and modified is very valuable.

7. REFERENCES

Barth, K. [1977] Zur Implementierung eines Lehrsystems für LISP. MA-Thesis, Inst. f. Informatik, Univ. Stuttgart.

Barth, K. [1978] ATN-Com: Ein Compiler für erweiterte Übergangsnetze. MMK Memo 7, IfI, Univ. Stuttgart.

Bates, M. [1978] The Theory and Practice of Augmented Transition Network Grammars. In: L. Bolc (Ed.) Natural Language Communication with Computers. Springer-Verlag, Berlin.

Bawden, D., Greenblatt, R., Holloway, J., Knight, T., Moon, D. & Weinreb, D. [1979] The Lisp machine. In: P. Winston & R. Brown (Eds.) Artificial Intelligence: an MIT Perspective. Vol. 2, The MIT Press, Cambr., Ma.

Bobrow, D.G. and Fraser, J.B. [1969] An Augmented State Transition Network Analysis Procedure. Proc. IJCAI1, 557-567.

Bobrow, D. & Wegbreit, B. [1973] A Model and Stack Implementation of Multiple Environments. Comm. ACM 16, Vol. 10, 591-603.

Boyer, R.S. & Moore, J.S. [1979] A Computational Logic. Academic Press, New York.

Brown, J.S., Burton, R.R. & Bell, A.G. [1974] SOPHIE - a Sophisticated Instructional Environment for Teaching Electronic Troubleshooting. BBN Report 2790, Cambridge.

Burton, R.R. & Woods, W.A. [1976] A Compiling System for Augmented Transition Networks. Preprints of 6. COLING Univ. of Ottawa.

Burton, R.R. [1976] Semantic Grammar: An Engineering Technique for Constructing Natural Language Understanding Systems. BBN Report No. 3453, Cambridge.

Charniak, E., Riesbeck, C. & McDermott, D.V. [1980] Artificial Intelligence Programming. Lawrence Erlbaum Assoc., Hillsdayle, N.J.

Christaller, T. [1980] Manual für eine ATN-Programmiersprache. In: T. Christaller & D. Metzing (Eds.) Augmented Transition Network Grammatiken, Teil II, 173-208.

Laubsch, J. et. al. [1976] MacLisp Manual. MMK Memo 3, Institut für Informatik, Universität Stuttgart.

Laubsch, J. [1979] Interfacing a semantic net with an augmented transition network. Proc. of the 6th Intern. Joint Conf. on Artificial Intelligence, 516-8, Tokio.

Laubsch, J. [1980] Leitfaden zum Entwerfen semantischer Grammatiken. In: T. Christaller & D. Metzing (Eds.) Augmented Transition Network Grammatiken. (Band 2). Einhorn Verlag, Berlin.

Laubsch, J. & Roesner, D. [1980] Active schemata and their role in semantic parsing. COLING 80, Tokio.

Moon, D. [1978] MacLisp Reference Manual, Parts 1, 2, 3 (revised edition). MIT Laboratory for Computer Science, Cambridge.

Rathke, C. & Sonntag, B. [1979] Einsatz semantischer Grammatiken in Frage/Antwortsystemen. MA Thesis, IfI, Univ. Stuttgart.

Schank, R.C. (Ed.) [1975] Conceptual Information Processing. North Holland, Amsterdam.

Simmons, R.F. & Bennet-Novak, G. [1975] Semantically Analyzing an English Subset for the Clown's Microworld, AJCL Microfiche 18.

Stallman, R.M. [1979] EMACS: The Extensible Customizable, Self-Documenting Display Editor. MIT Artificial Intelligence Laboratory, Memo 519, Cambridge, USA.

Steele, G.L. [1977] Debunking the "Expensive Procedure Call" Myth or, Procedure Call Implementations considered Harmful or, Lambda: the Ultimate Goto. MIT Artificial Intelligence Laboratory Memo 443.

Steele, G.L. & Sussmann, G.J. [1979] Design of LISP-Based Processors or, SCHEME: A Dielectric LISP or, Finite Memories Considered Harmful or, LAMBDA: The Ultimate Opcode. MIT Artificial Intelligence Laboratory Memo 514.

Teitelman, W. [1972] Automated Programmering - The Programmer's
    Assistant. Proceedings of the Fall Joint Computer Conference.

Weinreb, D. & Moon, D. [1981] Lisp Machine Manual. Third Edition, MIT
    Artificial Intelligence Laboratory, Cambridge, Mass.

Weyrauch, R.W. [1977] A Users Manual for FOL. Stanford Artificial
    Intelligence Laboratory Memo 235.

Winston, P.H., Horn, B.K. [1981] Lisp. Addison Wesley Publ. Co.,
    Reading, Ma.

Woods, W.A. [1970] Transition Network Grammars for Natural Language
    Analysis. CACM 13, 591-606.

Woods, W.A. et. al. [1976] Speech Understanding Systems. Final Report,
    Vol. 5: Trip, BBN Rep. 3438. Bolt, Beranek & Newman, Cambr., Ma.

Woods, W.A. [1977] Semantics and Quantification in Natural Language
    Question Answering. BBN Report No. 3687. Bolt, Beranek & Newman,
    Cambridge, Ma.

Woods, W.A. [1978] Generalizations of ATN Grammars. In: Research in
    Natural Language Understanding, BBN Rep. No. 3963, Bolt, Beranek
    & Newman, Cambridge, Ma.

Towards the Elastic ATN Implementation

Krzysztof Kochut[1]

CONTENTS

---

[1] Institute of Informatics
Warsaw University
PKIN, pok. 850
00-901 WARSZAWA / Poland

1.0 INTRODUCTION

Augmented Transition Network Grammars, as described by Woods [Woods, 1970], are designed mainly for the needs of natural language recognition. This mechanism seems to be very useful in the whole complex process, ranging from creation of words from phonemes obtained from the special phonetic device, to lexical analysis, syntactic structures creation, and finally semantic interpretation of the natural language sentences being examined.

However, the most common application of ATN grammars is in natural language access to information retrieving systems. In this case it is usually possible to limit the desired subset of the language being recognized. Such a limitation affects the way grammar is written and results in the creation of more semantic grammars.

As we know, such an approach has a significant disadvantage. Once written, the grammar for a system is always connected with it. There is no possibility of using the grammar in any other system.

In our project, called 'Dialog' at Warsaw University's Institute of Informatics, we decided to use ATN grammars as the natural language component. However, our system was designed as a meta-system, or basic system, that can be quickly oriented to different domains of knowledge. (Current efforts are concentrated on the creation of systems to retrieve legal files and to analyze medical publications.)

As we wanted to limit difficulties connected with changing the domain of knowledge (I mean troubles in changing the language subset) we had to prepare a fairly elastic implementation of ATN grammars.

The natural language module was essentially divided into two parts: syntactical and semantical. Both parts were realized by separate ATN grammars. Our goal was to obtain a basic system that could be adapted easily to a new domain by changing only the semantical part. Choosing the appropriate implementation, which had to be very effective and give as much information as possible, was of thus great importance.

With these requirements in mind, the application of a slightly modified Earley's algorithm [Earley, 1970] seemed very interesting. It is characterized by providing all possible parsings (in one grammar) by proceeding along every path in parallel.

It has a great advantage in cases of languages with sentences of many parsings. Results obtained in the syntactical part may be analyzed in the semantical part of choosing the right result or stating that there is not any.

Another type of implementation which facilitates cooperation among the various parts of language analysis is the application of cascaded ATN grammars, as presented in [Woods, 1980]. Each part is realized by a separate stage in the cascade. This implementation seemed to be the most appropriate for our needs. Different constituents of the analysis may be consequent stages here. The final stages are assigned to mostly limited fields of knowledge. It allows easy adaptation of the base module to new tasks by changing only the last stages in the cascade.

The above-mentioned implementations have compilers to translate either all or part of the grammar into the machine code, providing a great improvement in execution speed.

Both compilers are incremental, i.e. in cases where part of the grammar is modified, recompilation of only the changed part, not the whole grammar, is necessary.

For efficient and easy grammar modification the special editor EDATN is used. The whole system is suitable for adapting the basic system to new domains of information retrieving systems.

It is highly probable that the methods presented here may also be applicable to linguistics, dialogue modelling and many other applications.

The functions are coded in slightly modified LISP 1.5. Some functions from Interlisp, Maclisp and LISPMACHINELISP are included. A notation similar to Backus-Naur formalism is used.

2.0 DEFINITION OF THE ATN

The definition of the ATN presented here is not a formal one and is limited to a subset used in this work. The complete definition may be found in [Woods, 1970] or [Bates, 1978].

ATN can be described briefly as a finite state automaton equipped with

the additional capability of keeping contextual information in special
variables, called registers, and also of recursively invoking other automata of the same kind. Quite often ATN has a special store, named
HOLDLIST, that may be referenced everywhere in the automaton.

Therefore, ATN is the set of states connected in the network with directed arcs. The arcs may be any of the following types:

1. (CAT <category> <test> <actions> (TO <next-state>))

    The CAT arc may be taken if the current input word has the
    lexical <category> and <test> evaluates to non-NIL. Then
    <actions> are performed (from left to right) and a transition
    to <next-state> is executed through special action TO.

2. (WRD <word> <test> <actions> (TO <next-state>))

    The WRD arc may be used if the current input element matches
    the <word>. Then <actions> and transition to <next-state> are
    performed.

3. (PUSH <state> <test> <pre-actions> <post-actions> (TO <next-state>))

    If <test> gives the true value then <pre-actions> are evaluated
    and a transition to <state>, usually in another subnet, is per-
    formed. After executing the corresponding POP arc a return is
    made and <post-actions> along with transition to <next-state>
    are evaluated. The register association list is cleared before
    transition to <state>.

4. (POP <form> <test> <actions>)

    The function of this arc is to evaluate the <actions> after
    <test> has been satisfied. Then the special variable * is
    bound to the evaluated <form> and a return to the corresponding
    PUSH arc is made.
    When there is no corresponding PUSH arc, a return to the top
    level is executed.
    Note that POP arc has no destination state.

5. (JUMP <state> <test> <actions>)

    This kind of arc results in a transition to the <state>, pro-
    vided that <test> is satisfied. At the same time <actions> are
    evaluated.

6.   (VIR <const-type> <test> <actions> (TO <next-state>))

A VIR-type arc can be taken if <test> is satisfied and there
is one element in the store HOLDLIST, labelled <const-type>,
which is removed from the store and a variable * is bound to it.
Then <actions> and transition are executed.

After the evaluation of the first two arcs (CAT, WRD), the current input word is advanced. On the remaining arcs the current input word is
unchanged.

In order to get or set information to the registers or the HOLDLIST a
number of actions are available. Among them are:

- (SETR <register> <value>)

   This binds the named <register> with new <value>.

- (ADDR <register> <value>)

   This adds the new <value> to the right end of the actual
   <register> 's contents (treated as a list).

- (GETR <register>)

   This returns the actual value of <register>.

- (HOLD <const-type> <form>)

   This evaluates the <form> and then stores it marked as
   <const-type> in the HOLDLIST.

Any LISP atom may be used as a <register> and <const-type> and any LISP
form as a <form> and <value>. The variable LEX is bound to the current
input element.

The variable * is bound to the value of LEX on the JUMP, POP and WRD arcs;
on the CAT arc it is bound to the root form of the current word; on the
VIR arc it is bound to the element just picked up from HOLDLIST; on the
PUSH arc the variable * is bound to the value of LEX while evaluating
pre-actions; then it is bound to the form just POPped.

(VERIFY <form>) action is a very useful tool. It can play a role of an
additional test on arc: if the <form> evaluates to NIL then the analysis
with that arc is stopped.

Certainly the set of arcs and actions may be expanded for the needs of a real system. Many arc types and many actions are omitted here, since the readability of the functions presented would otherwise become rather difficult.

Several interesting arcs and actions can be found in [Bates, 1978], where is also a valuable example of the ATN grammar for English.

3.0 IMPLEMENTATION OF ATN BASED ON EARLEY's ALGORITHM

The first type of ATN implementation I would like to present is one based on Earley's well-known algorithm for parsing context-free languages.

T.W. Finin, in his report [Finin, 1977], described another implementation which used a 'depth-first-search' strategy. After successful transition through the network only one parse of the sentence being examined can be obtained. To get the remaining parsings several backtracks must be made.

Application of Earley's algorithm gives us a completely different way of performing the analysis. As originally defined [Earley, 1970] it was intended for context-free languages recognition and thus needs some adaptations for our requirements. Many data structures to keep register contents, HOLDLIST, etc. have to be implemented.

3.1 Earley's Algorithm

The trick to this algorithm lies in running the analysis of the input string in parallel, using all possible paths in the grammar. It is achieved by constructing the sets of states describing the actual situation in the parsing process. New sets are created along with advancing of the current input element.

The members of these sets are special states carrying the information about the production currently in use, the position in this production, the position in the input string where we started matching the production, and a string of k 'look-ahead' symbols.

Let the state be the quadruple

(p,j,f,α) ,where

p = production in use

j = position in this production (it is similar to the
function of a dot in LR(k) parsers - see for example
[Aho, Ullman, 1972])

f = position in the input string

α = string of k 'look-ahead' symbols.

I will now try to explain the way in which sets of states are to be created. Initially, the new set, let it be S, which includes only one state
is created. The state describes the initial situation of the parser and
thus looks like

$(\phi->S\cancel{S},0,0,\cancel{S}^k)$ where

$\cancel{S}$ is the symbol not in the set of grammar symbols, and $\phi->S\cancel{S}$ is the
production added only for analysis requirements. S is the start symbol
of the grammar.

After that we apply one of the actions described below to each state in
the set.

The three actions are the SCANNER, the PREDICTOR and the COMPLETER. The
purpose of these actions is as follows:

The SCANNER is used when the next symbol in the production, just in
front of a dot, is a terminal symbol equal to the one which is the current element of the input string. Its function is to add the state of
the form

$(p,j+1,f,\alpha)$ to the next set;

in fact it results in moving the dot to the position immediately following the matched terminal symbol.

The PREDICTOR is applied if the next symbol in the production is a non-
terminal one. We add the state of the form

$(q,0,i,\delta)$

to the end of the list of elements in the current set. Here q is a production with the encountered symbol on its left side, i is the number

of the current set, and δ belongs to $FIRST_k(\beta\alpha)$, where β is the remaining part of the production p. $FIRST_k(\beta\alpha)$ is the set of strings, composed of at most k terminal symbols which begin the strings derivable from βα. The formal definition may be found in [Earley, 1970] or in [Aho, Ullman, 1972]. Note that there may be many states of the above form.

The COMPLETER is used if the dot reaches the right end of the production (it means that we have recognized the string derivable from the production p). The string α has to match the next k input symbols as well; in this case we look through the f-th set searching for the states of the form

$$(q,1,m,\beta)$$

in which the dot is placed just before the symbol identical to that of the left side of the production p. For every such state we add a new state of the form

$$(q,1+1,m,\beta) \qquad \text{to the current set.}$$

Thus, applying one of these three actions results in adding states to the current set or to the next set. After the current set of states is exhausted we give the next set the name of the current one, initializing the new, empty set. We also advance the input string.

If the next set appears to be empty then the string being examined is underivable in the grammar. But if the next set consists only of one state of the form

$$(\phi->S\not{S},2,0,\not{S})$$

and the input string is exhausted then we can state that the input string is derivable in the given grammar.

When the grammar is ambiguous then there may be many parsings of the input string, but only one if the grammar is non-ambiguous.

Any example of a parsing using the original algorithm would not be very interesting and will not be presented here. Interested readers are encouraged to consult Earley's above-mentioned work.

As we notice the process of analysis can be viewed as a wave moving through every possible derivation in the grammar.

3.2 Adaptation of Earley's Algorithm to the ATN

It appears that Earley's algorithm can be easily adapted to the needs of ATN grammars.

The main idea remains unchanged: the ATN net should be examined with the use of every possible path in this grammar. The analysis proceeds up to the last POP at the top level (there may be many POPs before we reach the lop level due to many possible parsings).

Each state in the network explicitly describes the path and the position in it. This corresponds to the production currently being used and the position of a dot in it. There is one exception, however. It is possible that an ATN state may be obtained 'at the same moment' from two separate but different states. In fact, these states represent different paths despite the fact that they meet at the same state. As we can see below this is not a serious disadvantage.

Notice that each ATN state has its own environment. It has to have its own register association list and a HOLDLIST. Thus the form of a state to be kept in a set of states (in Earley's sense) is as follows:

('ATN-state' 'its-own-REGS' 'its-own-HOLDLIST').*

Data structures are necessary for the register association list and the HOLDLIST, but there is no need for keeping much information that is essential to backtracking. After all each alternative is tried immediately and used if possible.

There is no need for a real PUSH. It decreases the amount of information required to reconstruct the configuration after returning in great part.

In the original algorithm when a dot immediately precedes a non-terminal symbol we remember the index of a set in which a state with such production was noticed. It obviously corresponds to the PUSH in terms of the ATN. In this case we must ensure the possibility of a return. The original method may be used here but it is inefficient for two reasons:

---

* In fact, the state in a set is represented by a list of four elements. The role of the last, additional element is connected with the presence of PUSH arc and will be explained later.

First, each set of states should be maintained during the whole analysis. It would be memory space consuming especially if a very large network is being used.

Second, searching for the right state using the normal list structures would be time consuming.

As we want to avoid such difficulties, all necessary information is placed on the property list of one atom (unique to one analysis). This atom is itself a fourth element in the state list.

One bit of that information is an atom with the same purpose. The information of the same kind but of a higher level is placed on its property list. Then a kind of a chain is created that reflects a consequent descent to subnets (subcomputations). If such a solution is applied then only two sets of states are needed: the set currently being processed and the subsequent one.

The fourth element in a state (in Earley's sense) is a string of k 'look-ahead' symbols. It is used when a dot reaches the right end of some production to determine the successful application of that production. In our case it corresponds to finishing the analysis in one subnet. In fact it is similar to executing a POP arc. But this kind of arc is taken only if a test on it is satisfied, which is why we do not need to implement the 'look-ahead' mechanism.

The analysis is finished if the next set of states is empty.

The initial state consists of the state that is an entry point to the network, an empty register association list, an empty HOLDLIST, and NIL (indicating that there is no corresponding PUSH).

3.3 Example of an Analysis

The example to be demonstrated here will be a little artificial, for presenting one based on natural sentence analysis (with more than one parsing) would be tiresome and take up too much space. I think that the one below is quite sufficient for illustrating the function of the algorithm.

The grammar used is shown in figure 1.

```
(SUBNET X
   (X    (WRD  A T (HOLD 'X1 *) (TO X1))
         (PUSH Y T (SETR P3 *) (TO X7))
         (PUSH Z T (SETR P1 *) (TO X10)))
   (X1   (WRD A T (HOLD 'X2 *) (TO X2)))
   (X2   (WRD B T (SETR P1 *) (TO X3)))
   (X3   (VIR X1 T (SETR P2 *) (TO X4)))
   (X4   (WRD B T (SETR P3 *) (TO X5)))
   (X5   (VIR X2 T (SETR P4 *) (TO X6)))
   (X6   (POP (MAPCAR '(P1 P2 P3 P4) (FUNCTION GETR))))
   (X7   (WRD B T (SETR P1 *) (TO X8)))
   (X8   (WRD B T (SETR P2 *) (TO X9)))
   (X9   (POP (APPEND (LIST (GETR P1) (GETR P2)) (GETR P3))))
   (X10 (POP (GETR P1))) )

(SUBNET Y
   (Y    (WRD A T (ADDR P1 *) (TO Y1)))
   (Y1   (WRD A T (ADDR P1 *) (TO Y1))
         (JUMP Y2))
   (Y2   (POP (GETR P1))) )

(SUBNET Z
   (Z    (WRD A T (SETR P1 *) (TO Z1)))
   (Z1   (PUSH Z T (SETR P2 *) (TO Z2))
         (JUMP Z2)))
   (Z2   (WRD B T (SETR P3 *) (TO Z3)))
   (Z3   (POP (APPEND (APPEND (GETR P2) (LIST (GETR P1)))
                       (LIST (GETR P3)) ))) )
```

Fig. 1: Grammar Example

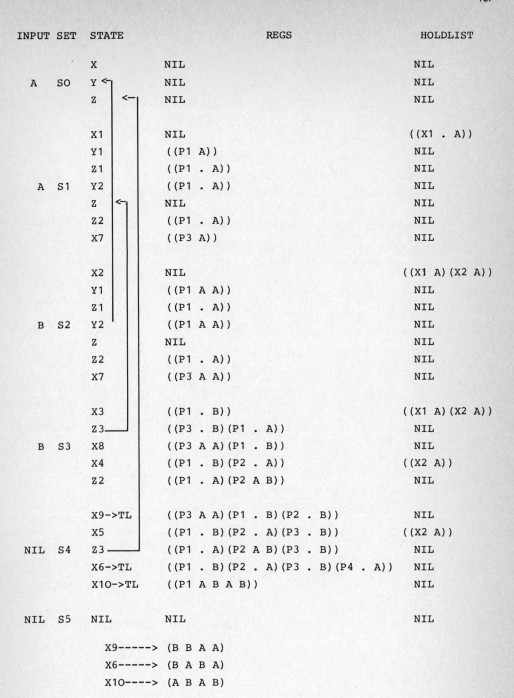

```
INPUT SET   STATE                    REGS                      HOLDLIST

            X          NIL                                     NIL
  A    SO   Y          NIL                                     NIL
            Z          NIL                                     NIL


            X1         NIL                                     ((X1 . A))
            Y1         ((P1 A))                                NIL
            Z1         ((P1 . A))                              NIL
  A    S1   Y2         ((P1 . A))                              NIL
            Z          NIL                                     NIL
            Z2         ((P1 . A))                              NIL
            X7         ((P3 A))                                NIL


            X2         NIL                                     ((X1 A)(X2 A))
            Y1         ((P1 A A))                              NIL
            Z1         ((P1 . A))                              NIL
  B    S2   Y2         ((P1 A A))                              NIL
            Z          NIL                                     NIL
            Z2         ((P1 . A))                              NIL
            X7         ((P3 A A))                              NIL


            X3         ((P1 . B))                              ((X1 A)(X2 A))
            Z3         ((P3 . B)(P1 . A))                      NIL
  B    S3   X8         ((P3 A A)(P1 . B))                      NIL
            X4         ((P1 . B)(P2 . A))                      ((X2 A))
            Z2         ((P1 . A)(P2 A B))                      NIL


            X9->TL     ((P3 A A)(P1 . B)(P2 . B))              NIL
            X5         ((P1 . B)(P2 . A)(P3 . B))              ((X2 A))
  NIL  S4   Z3         ((P1 . A)(P2 A B)(P3 . B))              NIL
            X6->TL     ((P1 . B)(P2 . A)(P3 . B)(P4 . A))      NIL
            X10->TL    ((P1 A B A B))                          NIL


  NIL  S5   NIL        NIL                                     NIL


            X9-----> (B B A A)
            X6-----> (B A B A)
            X10----> (A B A B)


     Fig. 2: Analysis Example
```

Look at the analysis of the string AABB. Expending a little effort to examine figure 2 will be the best way to understand the function of the algorithm.

Individual steps in the analysis are presented. The PUSH arcs are connected to the corresponding POP arcs with arrows. The arrows pointing to TL signs reflect execution of POP arcs at the top level. Three results of the analysis are shown underneath.

Consequent sets of states are separated. States in sets are processed sequentially. In the columns headed REGS and HOLDLIST you can find the subsequent values of register association list and HOLDLIST respectively.

3.4 Implementation of the Parser

In this section an example of ATN grammar implementation based on the algorithm presented in sec. 3.2 will be given. Functions listed here include only the most important fragments.

3.4.1 Main Functions of the Interpreter

The top level function is the monitor. It governs the processing of states from the set as well as movement through the list of sets. It also initializes and finishes the work of the parser.

```
(PARSE (LAMBDA (STRING STATE)
    (PROG (CURR-SET NEXT-SET PARSELIST S-A S-H)
        ... ...
        (SET (SETQ S-A (GENSYM 'REGS)) NIL)
        (SET (SETQ S-H (GENSYM 'HOLD)) NIL)
        (SETQ NEXT-SET (INIT-SET))
        (ADD-TO-SET (LIST STATE S-A S-H NIL) NEXT-SET)
  NEXT  (SETQ CURR-SET NEXT-SET)
        (SETQ NEXT-SET (INIT-SET))
        (PROCESS_SET)
        (COND ((EMPTY_SET? NEXT-SET)
                  (COND ((END_OF_SENTENCE?)
                            (RETURN PARSELIST))
                       (T (RETURN 'FAIL))) ))
        (GO NEXT)
        ... ...      )))
```

The function ADD-TO-SET adds the state which is the first argument to the end of the list of states of the set which is the second argument.

The meaning of functions END_OF_SENTENCE? and EMPTY_SET? is obvious.

Function of no argument PROCESS_SET processes the states in the subsequent sets. Variables * and LEX are bound by the function GET_NEXT_WORD which returns the next input element.

```
(PROCESS_SET (LAMBDA NIL
    (PROG ( * LEX)
     ... ...
        (SETQ LEX (GET_NEXT_WORD STRING))
        (SETQ  * LEX)
NEXT_STATE
        (OR (LAST_STATE?) (RETURN T))
        (PROCESS_STATE (GET_NEXT_STATE))
        (GO NEXT_STATE) )))
```

GET_NEXT_STATE returns the next state of the set currently being processed.

PROCESS_STATE is responsible for checking the ATN state. If it is part of a compiled grammar an appropriate function is applied; otherwise the interpreter is invoked.

```
(PROCESS_STATE (LAMBDA (STATE)
    (COND ((OR (GET (CAR STATE) 'EXPR)
               (GET (CAR STATE) 'SUBR))
            (EVAL STATE))
          (T (APPLY 'EVAL_STATE
                (CONS (CAR STATE)
                    (MAPCAR (CDR STATE) 'EVAL)))))))
```

Notice that the form of the state kept in a set is in fact an s-expression. This allows us to invoke very easily the function realizing the ATN state.

The function EVAL_STATE retrieves the arcs leaving the state and tries to process them sequentially. Each kind of arc is operated by a special function. The basic parts of the function are shown below.

Every state in a set should have its own environment defined. Variables S-A and S-H are bound to names unique to one analysis. These names are

in turn bound to the register association list and the HOLDLIST proper
to that state.

This is a slightly artificial situation, necessary for the following
reasons: the resulting new environment (after performing the actions
placed on the arc) could not be bound to the atoms REGS and HOLD respectively because each remaining arc evaluated in EVAL_STATE should have
the same, unchanged environment. Accordingly, the new data structures
(created after evaluating the actions on the arc) are pointed to by
atoms that remain unknown to the functions realizing SETR and HOLD actions, making the use of some kind of indirection necessary.

```
(EVAL_STATE (LAMBDA (STATE REGS HOLD CONT)
    (PROG (ARC_TYPE TEST ARCS)
       ... ...
       (SETQ ARCS (GET_ARCS STATE))
   AGN (COND ((NULL ARCS) (RETURN T)))
       (SET (SETQ S-A (GENSYM 'REGS)) REGS)
       (SET (SETQ S-H (GENSYM 'HOLD)) HOLD)
       (SETQ ARC_TYPE (CAAR ARCS))
       (SETQ TEST (COND ((CDDAR ARCS) (CADDAR ARCS))
                        (T T)))
       (AND (EVAL TEST)
            (SELECT ARC_TYPE
                ('CAT    (DO_CAT  ...))
                ('WRD    (DO_WRD  ...))
                ... ... ...
                ('VIR    (DO_VIR  ...)) NIL))
       (SETQ ARCS (CDR ARCS))
       (GO AGN) )))
```

The special functions that realize the various arcs will be presented.
Argument lists are identical and take the form

```
(HEAD TEST ACTIONS CONTIN)
```

1. DO_WRD realizes WRD arc. The main fragment of the code is as follows

```
(OR (EQ HEAD *) (RETURN NIL))
(MAPC ACTIONS (FUNCTION EVAL))
(RETURN (ADD-TO-SET
            (LIST NEXT_STATE S-A S-H
                 (LIST 'QUOTE CONTIN)) NEXT-SET))
```

The variable NEXT_STATE is bound to the function realizing the ATN action TO.

2. DO_CAT is activated when a cat arc is to be processed.

It is very similar to the previous DO_WRD function. The only difference is the additional test due to the specific meaning of the CAT arc.

```
(OR (SETQ * (CATCHECK HEAD))
    (RETURN (SETQ * LEX)))
```

The above two arcs are equivalent to the operation SCANNER by means of consuming the current input word and adding something to the next set.

The operation PREDICTOR is equivalent to the call of the lower subnet instead. We have to add the start state of a subcomputation to the current set (do not advance the input here) to start going through the subnet.

In order to ensure return to the higher subnet we place the list of special operations on the property list of an atom unique to one analysis. After performing these operations we return to the higher subnet. In EVAL_STATE the variable CONT is bound to such an atom. It is also the fourth element of the state in the set.

3. DO_PUSH realizes PUSH arc.

```
(SETQ NEXT_CONTIN (GENSYM 'CONT))
(SET (SETQ X (GENSYM 'REGS)) REGS)
(SET (SETQ Y (GENSYM 'HOLD)) HOLD)
(SET S-A (SET S-H NIL))
(PUT NEXT_CONTIN
      `((SETQ S-A (QUOTE ,X))
        (SETQ S-H (QUOTE ,Y))
        ,@ACTIONS
        (ADD-TO-SET (LIST NEXT_STATE S-A S-H
                          (LIST 'QUOTE (QUOTE ,CONTIN)))))
      'CNT)
```

The above code fragment is written with the use of the backquote facility, similar to that in LISPMACHINELISP [Weinreb, Moon, 1979].

4. DO_POP realizes the POP arc. The POP arc cooperates with the PUSH.

The variable * is bound to the evaluated form, whereupon we decide where to return. If CONTIN is not NIL then the corresponding PUSH arc is executed, otherwise the current path is completed.

In the first case much work has already been done by the DO_PUSH function.

```
(SETQ * (EVAL HEAD))
(MAPC ACTIONS (FUNCTION EVAL))
(COND (CONTIN (PROG2
                (MAPC (GET CONTIN 'CNT)
                      (FUNCTION EVAL))
                (RETURN (SETQ * LEX)) ))
      (T (SETQ PARSELIST
            (APPEND PARSELIST (CONS * NIL)))))
(SETQ * LEX)
```

The POP arc is similar in meaning to the COMPLETER operation in Earley's algorithm.

The remaining arcs, namely JUMP and VIR, are quite different from any of Earley's three operations.

5. DO_JUMP realizes the JUMP arc.

Main fragments of the code:

```
(MAPC ACTIONS (FUNCTION EVAL))
(ADD-TO-SET (LIST HEAD S-A S-H (LIST 'QUOTE CONTIN))
            CURR-SET)
```

6. DO_VIR is invoked by the VIR arc.

An additional test has to be included.

```
(OR (SETQ * (GET_HOLD HEAD))
    (RETURN (SETQ * LEX)))
(MAPC ACTIONS (FUNCTION EVAL))
(SETQ * LEX)
(ADD-TO-SET (LIST NEXT_STATE S-A S-H (LIST 'QUOTE CONTIN))
            CURR-SET)
```

The function GET_HOLD scans the HOLDLIST searching for an element of the
required type. If there is such an element the function returns after
removing it from HOLDLIST. Otherwise it returns NIL.

The three functions DO_CAT, DO_POP and DO_VIR change the value of *. It
should be restored each time.

The variable PARSELIST contains every possible parsing. If no parsing
is possible the system returns the atom FAIL.

I should say a few words about set organization. The four functions
GET_NEXT_STATE, EMPTY_SET?, LAST_STATE? and ADD-TO-SET are used to operate sets of states. The addition of an element to the set will be the
most frequent operation, of course. The states are added to the end of
a list of states in the set. Thus, having a pointer to the last element
of the list is very profitable. The set may then be organized as follows:

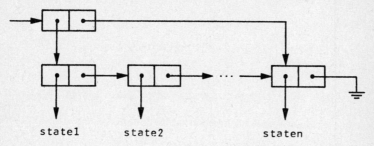

To create such a structure the use of the function TCONC, similar to
that found in Interlisp (see for example [Haraldson, 1975]), seems to
be the most appropriate. With the help of this function, adding states
to sets can be accomplished very quickly.

3.4.2 Realization of ATN Actions

Only the realization of the most important actions will be described
here. The most common are: SETR, GETR, and HOLD. In addition, several
other actions such as ADDR, ADDL, SENDR, LIFTR, VERIFY or BUILDQ are
frequently realized in ATN systems. A variety of actions to retrieve
lexical information is usually provided as well.

As I have already mentioned functions realizing access to the register
association list and HOLDLIST do not 'know' in what ATN state they are
executed. Thus the implementation must provide it.

Functions SETR and GETR are of the type FEXPR.

1. (SETR <register-name> <value>)
```
        (SETQ REGS
                (SET S-A (CONS (CONS REGNAME (EVAL VALUE))
                                REGS)))
```

2. (GETR <register-name>)
```
        (CDR (COND ((SETQ VAL (ASSOC REGNAME REGS))
                        VAL)
                   (T '(NIL))))
```

The additional binding of the variable REGS must be executed. Otherwise, evaluation of several SETRs on the same arc would result in adding the effect of only the last SETR. Notice that the register association list resulting from these SETR actions must be the binding of an atom unique to one analysis!

The variables REGS and HOLD are bound to the function EVAL_STATE.

3. (HOLD <const-type> <form>)

    The HOLD action is implemented very similarly; it is, however, of the type EXPR.
```
        (SETQ HOLD
                (SET S-H
                        (CONS (LIST C_TYPE FORM)
                                HOLD)))
```

Realization of the action VERIFY is also worth mentioning. It requires the CATCH-THROW mechanism found in MacLisp. Its purpose is to perform non-local exits. To provide the above action we should enclose the SE-LECT function (in EVAL_STATE) in the CATCH. It may look like
```
        (CATCH
            (SELECT ARC_TYPE
                ... ... ...
                NIL)
            EVAL_ARC)
```

Then the VERIFY action could be of the form
```
        (VERIFY (LAMBDA (FORM)
            (OR FORM (THROW NIL EVAL_ARC)) ))
```

Executing the above THROW will make the control move immediately to the s-expression which follows the CATCH in EVAL_STATE. The next arc will then be tried without continuing the current one.

3.4.3 Compiler of ATN Grammars

The ATN grammar compiler speeds up the analysis of a given sentence.

It is achieved by changing part of the grammar to several LISP functions. These functions may then be compiled by the LISP system to a machine code, resulting in a great improvement in the execution speed.

Each state of the grammar is translated into one LISP function. Application of such a function is equivalent to performing tries on every arc leaving the state and evaluating them.

The compiler must ensure the semantical equivalence of the generated function and the state that has been compiled.

The entire grammar may be compiled to a machine code as well, which speeds the analysis up considerably. There should be no difference in the functioning of the system for the user.

The above model of grammar compilation allows for easy modification of the network. After the grammar has been changed there is no need to re-compile the whole grammar, only modified fragments of it. If a suitable editor is supplied as well, then the problem of testing and debugging the grammar is greatly facilitated.

The compiler itself is written with the use of the top-down, recursive descent method. It is very simple and will not be described here.

The scheme of the function generated by the compiler is as follows:

```
(state-name (LAMBDA (REGS HOLD CONTIN)
    (PROG (NEXT_STATE NEXT_CONTIN)
        code for arc 1
        code for arc 2
        ... ... ...
        code for arc n )))
```

The code generated for particular arcs is very similar to the functions that realize them interpretatively.

The effect of compilation is shown in the following example. The code
presented here is the one generated for the state X of the grammar example in sec. 3.3.

```
(X (LAMBDA (REGS HOLD CONTIN)
    (PROG (NEXT_STATE NEXT_CONTIN)
        (AND (EQ *'A) T      ;test from the arc
            (PROGN (SET (SETQ S-A (GENSYM 'REGS)) REGS)
                (SET (SETQ S-H (GENSYM 'HOLD)) HOLD)
                (HOLD 'X1 * )
                (ADD-TO-SET (LIST 'X1 S-A S-H
                                (LIST 'QUOTE CONTIN))
                        NEXT-SET) ))
        (AND T
            (PROGN (SET (SETQ S-A (GENSYM 'REGS)) REGS)
                (SET (SETQ S-H (GENSYM 'HOLD)) HOLD)
                (PREPARE_RETURN)
                (ADD-TO-SET (LIST 'X7 S-A S-H
                                (LIST 'QUOTE CONTIN))
                        CURR-SET) ))
        (AND T
            (PROGN (SET (SETQ S-A (GENSYM 'REGS)) REGS)
                (SET (SETQ S-H (GENSYM 'HOLD)) HOLD)
                (PREPARE_RETURN)
                (ADD-TO-SET (LIST 'X1O S-A S-H
                                (LIST 'QUOTE CONTIN))
                        CURR-SET) ))  )))
```

The code for the generated function is not an optimal one (see the construction (AND T ...)). One may write a suitable optimizer and eliminate poor constructions such as this. The generated function will try
to take each arc of state X sequentially. If the arc can be taken, all
necessary actions will then be executed.

The function PREPARE_RETURN puts all necessary information to return
from subcomputation on the property list of the atom unique to one analysis.

3.5. Conclusion

The implementation presented here has the advantage of giving all possible parsings of the sentence being examined.

However, there is also one main disadvantage: if the automaton is highly undeterministic, the algorithm will produce many completely useless results.

In many LISP systems atoms generated by GENSYM may clutter up the free cell space. To avoid this we can clean the memory between subsequent analysis.

The realization of a lexicon, of no importance here, has been ignored. The reader can find some interesting ideas in [Cercone, Mercer, 1980].

4.0 IMPLEMENTATION OF CASCADED ATN GRAMMARS

The mechanism of cascaded ATN grammars is a kind of generalization of 'normal' ATN grammars.

4.1 Idea of a Cascaded ATN

The conception of a cascaded ATN has its origin in the observation of the HWIM (Hear What I Mean) - system implemented in the years 1974-1976 [Woods et.al., 1976].

Two components - lexical and pragmatical - cooperated there. The first was used to transform the stream of phonemes coming from the acoustic device to words. The latter used these words in the pragmatic grammar. The pragmatic grammar was driven by special tests and actions based on the semantic-pragmatic knowledge.

Unfortunately, the grammar designed for that system could only be used for the strictly defined environment (domain of knowledge) for which it was written. The adaptation of that grammar to other domains requires rewriting almost the entire grammar.

The grammar written in this manner was of immense size. The final version included more than 400 states and almost 900 arcs, which was of course space consuming.

The reason for its great size was simple: each syntactic element had many places in the grammar where it could be recognized because there were many semantic contexts in which that element could find its semantic interpretation. One could say that syntactic and semantic knowledge were mixed in the whole grammar.

The above-mentioned disadvantages inspired scientists to start decreasing the dependency of the grammar on the range of responsibility for which it was originally defined. In his reports, W. Woods [Woods, 1978] and [Woods, 1980] describes two ways of achieving this.

The first, called 'conceptual factoring', results in decreasing the number of places in the grammar in which the given syntactic fact must be represented.

The other, 'hypothesis factoring', decreases the number of different hypotheses tested during the process of analysis.

Both methods are realized through sharing the same facts or hypotheses in distinct places in the grammar.

The grammar on which 'conceptual factoring' was performed is more compact because each fact used in many places in the grammar had to be recognized only once. There is thus only one place in the grammar to represent that fact.

'Conceptual factoring' may be also achieved by providing only one place in the grammar to pick up facts that are not the same but similar with respect to their structure. Their differences are hidden in the registers. Some paths in the grammer sharing the same parts may be merged, thus resulting in 'conceptual factoring'.

'Conceptual factoring' decreases space requirements and also improves readability.

'Hypothesis factoring',on the other hand, improves the efficiency of the analysis. It is achieved by changing recursive calls to subnets to iteration. Strengthening of tests on arcs decreases indeterminism, which helps speed up the analysis as well. Performing several transformations of the network (treated as a finite state machine) is also possible.

Both methods are widely discussed in [Woods, 1980].

4.2 Cascaded ATN Grammars

Cascaded ATN grammar is in fact a sequence of almost ordinary networks (as defined for example in [Bates, 1978]). Component nets are wider than the normal ones only in that they contain an additional action TRANSMIT.

However, this action is crucial to the whole conception and it is used to operate communication between two neighboring grammars in the cascade.

Woods calls these grammars stages. The first stage takes the natural language sentence as its input and the last stage returns the effect of the whole cascade as its output. Each of the intermediate stages takes the output of the previous one as its input.

In other words, between the two neighboring stages there is a special buffer that is accessible only to that pair of stages. The first stage of the pair advances its results to the buffer and the next stage picks up those results as elements of its input.

The two methods of factoring described above are easily achieved in such a work organization. Let us examine it more closely. Many recognitions of facts commonly used further on may be shifted to early stages in the cascade; thus there is only one place where a given fact is picked up. The elements so recognized can then be used in many distinct contexts in subsequent stages.

Dividing the process of natural language recognition into phonology, vocabulary, syntactics, and semantics is very simple here. Each of these parts has its own stage in the cascade. Every time a new phoneme is required, the first stage TRANSMITs the new element just recognized to the next stage. The second stage then produces successive words composed of the obtained phonemes. Going on - the syntactic stage would construct subsequent syntactic phrases that could be used by the last, semantic stage, which could in turn perform some interpretation.

Such a division is also very suitable for testing and debugging the whole system. It is worth mentioning that the first three stages and a modified fourth are sufficient to make the adaptation of the existing basic system to the new domain of knowledge easy.

4.3 Ways of Implementing CATN

Let us see how this mechanism can be implemented. The whole operation and its effectivity depends to a great extent on the realization strategy used in the individual stages (grammars). Three different approaches to the solution of this problem will be presented.

Let us assume that each grammar is realized in a way similar to the one presented by Burton and Woods in [Burton, Woods, 1976]. Of course, the action TRANSMIT should be supplied, In this case, each stage would have to wait until the entire action of the previous one is complete. Activation of the next stage immediately after a TRANSMIT action has been executed would be impossible because we should secure the possibility of reactivating the previous stage in the place just following the TRANSMIT action. We would have to possess many entry points to the function generated for the grammar which realizes the given stage. Unfortunately, this is very difficult in many LISP dialects. The use of the 'depth-first-search' strategy has one main disadvantage: Suppose that the natural language sentence being examined has many different parsings and the first one (obtained with the use of 'depth-first-search' strategy) is not valid in the semantic interpretation. If the semantic stage fails on the first parsing, then the return (backtrack) to the previous stage to obtain the next parsing is impossible. Thus, the above approach would be of no use.

Another, more interesting possibility, is the use of the strategy based on Earley's algorithm (similar to that presented in the sec. 3.0).

Each stage would give every possible result for a given input after it has finished its work. The TRANSMIT operation would be reduced to transmitting each of its results to the output buffer. Every possible parsing would then be available, and if the next stage failed on the first parsing we would simply use another one. Activation of the previous stage would be unnecessary.

In this approach each stage may be treated as a separate part. It may be removed from the memory as soon as it finishes its work. Only the results must be saved. It is of great importance in cases of very large grammars.

The implementation of cascaded ATN grammars based on Earley's algorithm would be basically similar to the one presented in the previous paragraph. Only the special monitor governing the activation of every subsequent stage, buffers and their operation, and the action TRANSMIT should be added. Unfortunately this implementation is inefficient because it gives many useless results.

One more way of realizing CATN is the application of the algorithm proposed by W. Woods [Woods, 1980].

Each stage in the cascade is realized in the depth-first-search mode.
However, the proceedings in anyone stage are interrupted each time a
TRANSMIT action is executed. At that time the next stage is activated.
It would process the element just obtained from the previous stage. It
may in turn be interrupted by its own TRANSMIT operation or by the request of the next input element. In the latter case the previous stage
is activated in the place just following its last TRANSMIT. The working
of an ATNs cascade is shown below:

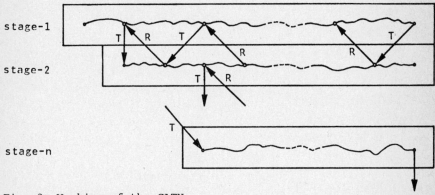

Fig. 3: Working of the CATN

In Fig. 3, the flow of control after execution of a TRANSMIT action is
shown as an arrow labelled with the letter T. Similarly, the flow of
control after a request of another input element is presented as an arrow labelled with the letter R.

Each stage remains idle after its TRANSMIT or request. The request of
the next stage or the TRANSMIT performed by the previous stage reacti-
vates it.

The next input element request is emitted after one of the consuming
arcs (such as CAT or WRD) has been taken. Communication between the two
neighboring stages is carried out through the special buffers to which
subsequent elements are added and from which they are picked up.

Each stage in the cascade is more or less an ordinary ATN and may thus
consist of several subnets. POP arcs may then be executed; the POP arc
to which there is no corresponding PUSH may also be taken. It is equivalent to going up to the top level of that stage. The analysis process
in that stage is finished and the next one activated with the POPed form
as its input.

Notice that POPs to the top level need not be taken in any stage but the last one. The cooperation may be organized in such a manner that a stage, together with the last TRANSMITted element, may also send a message that it is the last element. In this case, the analysis in this stage will not be reactivated.

To ensure correct functioning of this algorithm certain data structures must be implemented. Among them is a stack on which the subsequent configurations of one particular stage are pushed. It allows backtracking in the scope of that stage.

Another stack saves the subsequent configurations of the whole cascade (vector of the configurations of all stages). It allows us to backtrack in the scope of the whole cascade. Undoubtedly this is the strongest way of implementing the CATN.

It can happen that initiation the next stage of analysis requires completion of the previous one. In this case only one stack is necessary because there will be only one TRANSMIT executed; thus subsequent stages will be activated sequentially. In other words, the activation of stages will not be mixed.

4.4 Example of an Implementation

A general outline of the implementation of a cascaded ATN will be described here. The realization is based on the last of the methods discussed in sec. 4.3. The functions will be given in outline form only, as the full text would go beyond the limit of this work.

The main function is PARSE. It has two arguments: the name of the initial grammar and the sentence to be examined. It initiates some variables and invokes the function PROCESS_CATN. This function is in fact the interpreter of the CATN. It creates the list of stages in the cascade and then prepares the communication buffers (input buffer for the first grammar is initialized to the input sentence). Configurations of the stages are initialized as well.

```
(PROCESS_CATN (LAMBDA (START_ATN STRING)
    ... ... ...
    (ESTABLISH_BUFFERS ATN_VECTOR)
    (INIT_BUFFERS START_ATN STRING)
    (INIT_ATNS ATN_VECTOR)
    (SETQ ATN_NO 1)
```

```
   ON   (CATCH (ACTIVATE_ATN ATN_NO) ATN_CALL)
        (AND (NULL CATN_STACK) (RETURN 'FAIL))
        (AND (FINISHED_ALL? ATN_VECTOR)
              (RETURN RESULT))
        (GO ON)     )))
```

The meaning of the three functions ESTABLISH_BUFFERS, INIT_BUFFERS and
INIT_ATNS is obvious. If the stack CATN_STACK is empty (i.e. backtracking is impossible) the analysis fails. If each of the stages in the cascade has finished its work (function FINISHED_ALL?) then we may return
the RESULT of the analysis. If the analysis is not finished we must activate the next or the previous stage depending on the kind of interruption involved.

The variables *, LEX, STATE, REGS, HOLD and ATN_STACK are local in the
function ACTIVATE_ATN. ATN_STACK is a stack to keep subsequent configurations in the current stage to allow for backtracking.

```
     (ACTIVATE_ATN (LAMBDA (ATN_NO)
        ... ... ...
        (SET_LAST_CONF ATN_NO)
   NEXT (PROCESS_STATE STATE)
        (SETQ STATE NEXT_STATE)
        ... ... ...
        (GO NEXT)   ))
```

The function SET_LAST_CONF is used to spread the last active configuration of that stage (the variable STATE is also restored, among others).

The function PROCESS_STATE actually evaluates the given state. The 'normal' return from that function takes place only in the case of successful execution of an arc leaving that state. The variable NEXT_STATE is
bound in the TO action.

```
   (PROCESS_STATE (LAMBDA (STATE)
      ... ... ...
      (SETQ ARCS (GET_ARCS STATE))
  ARC (COND ((CATCH (PROCESS_ARC (CAR ARCS))
                 ARC_CALL)
              (RETURN (AND (CDR ARCS) (STORE_ATN_CONF)))))
      (SETQ ARCS (CDR ARCS))
```

```
      (AND ARCS (GO ARC))
      (BACKTRACK_ATN)
      (GO ARC)     ))
```

The function CATCH is used here to provide the proper functioning of
the action VERIFY. In case of successful evaluation of the arc the remaining alternative arcs are saved on ATN_STACK. Normal return from the
function BACKTRACK_ATN is performed only if there is another path in
the network to be tried. Otherwise, a return to the previous configuration of the cascade as a whole is to be made through evaluation of the
form

```
      (THROW NIL ATN_CALL)
```

In the end the function PROCESS_ARC will call a "special" function after recognition of the type of the given arc.

```
   (PROCESS_ARC (LAMBDA (ARC)
     ... ... ...
     (RETURN
       (PROG1
          (SELECT ARC_TYPE
             ('CAT    (DO_CAT ... ))
             .... .... ....
             ('VIR   (DO_VIR ... )) NIL)
          (AND INTERRUPT
             (INTERRUPT_ATN INTERRUPT)) ))
```

The interruption occurs if the TRANSMIT operation has been executed or
if the arc is of CAT or WRD type. The "special" functions realizing the
arcs are not very interesting and will not be discussed here. Instead
there are other functions which are very important. Let us look at them.

```
   (TO (LAMBDA (NEXT)
       (PROGN
          (COND (ADVANCE? (SETQ LEX (REQ_BUFF_CONT))))
          (SETQ * LEX)
          (SETQ NEXT_STATE NEXT)  )))
```

The switch ADVANCE? is set to T on the arcs CAT and WRD.

```
   (REQ_BUFF_CONT (LAMBDA NIL
       ... ... ...
```

```
(COND ((EMPTY_BUFF? INPUT)
           (PROG2 (SETQ INTERRUPT 'READ)
                  (GET_BUFF_CONT INPUT)))
       (T (GET_BUFF_CONT INPUT)))    ))
```

The variable INPUT points to the input buffer for the stage in which
the function REQ_BUFF_CONT is executed. Similarly, the variable OUTPUT
is itself a pointer to the output buffer of that stage. The functions
GET_BUFF_CONT and PUT_BUFF_CONT are used to read and write elements to
the buffers.

Where the input buffer is empty, the function REQ_BUFF_CONT returns a
pointer to its new 'free' element. That element is supplied with the
next element by PUT_BUFF_CONT. Thus, the variables LEX and * will at
first point to the free element in the buffer, but then to the correct
element.

```
(TRANSMIT (LAMBDA (FORM)
    (PROG2
        (PUT_BUFF_CONT FORM OUTPUT)
        (SETQ INTERRUPT 'TRANS) )))
```

The implementation of the buffers will not be discussed here.

The function INTERRUPT_ATN changes active stages, depending on the kind
of interruption. The next or the previous stage is activated. In both
cases we should save the current configuration of the CATN and then restore the last active configuration of the desired stage.

```
(INTERRUPT_ATN (LAMBDA (KIND)
    ... ... ...
    (STORE_CATN_VECTOR ATN_NO)
    (SETQ ATN_NO
        (COND ((EQ KIND 'TRANS) (ADD1 ATN_NO))
              (T (SUB1 ATN_NO))))
    (THROW T ATN_CALL)       ))
```

The function STORE_CATN_VECTOR saves the current configuration of the
cascade (including the current configuration of the stage that caused
the interruption). It allows for future backtracks in the cascade.

The last interesting function is the BACKTRACK_ATN. The function

RESTORE_CATN_VECTOR, used here, also restores the variable ATN_NO.

```
(BACKTRACK_ATN (LAMBDA NIL
      (COND (ATN_STACK
              (RESTORE_ATN_CONF))
            (T (PROG2
                 (RESTORE_CATN_VECTOR)
                 (THROW T ATN_CALL))))  ))
```

Many other functions must be included in the real system, among them.
Functions realizing ATN actions like SETR, ADDR, HOLD or GETR. Several
actions to retrieve lexical information should also be implemented, but
their realization is rather simple and will not be presented here.

4.5 Compiler of the CATN

The version of the CATN presented above does not include cooperation
with the compiled grammar. To do this we have to introduce several changes.

First of all, the function PROCESS_STATE should check to see whether
the given state is compiled or not. If so, the control should be given
to the function realizing that state (assuming that each state is transformed to one separate LISP function).

```
(PROCESS_STATE (LAMBDA (STATE)
   ... ... ...
 STATE (AND (OR (GET STATE 'EXPR)
               (GET STATE 'SUBR))
           (RETURN (APPLY STATE NIL)))
   ARC (COND ((CATCH (PROCESS_ARC (CAR ARCS))
                 ARC_CALL)
               (RETURN (PROG2 (AND (CDR ARCS)
                                   (STORE_ATN_CONF))
                             T))))
       (SETQ ARCS (CDR ARCS))
       (AND ARCS (GO ARC))
       (BACKTRACK_ATN)
       (GO STATE)
```

The scheme of the function generated for a state has to allow skipping
arcs that have already been tried. This situation may occur after the
backtrack.

```
(state-name (LAMBDA NIL
    ... ... ...
    (OR ARCS (GO ARC1))
    (BRANCH (ARC1 ARC2 ...  ARCn) (CAR ARCS))
    ARC1   code for arc 1
    ARC2   code for arc 2
    ... ... ...
    ARCn   code for arc n   ))
```

The form of the BRANCH function is as follows:

```
(BRANCH label-list s-expression)
```

The s-expression should evaluate to the number in the range from 1 to the number of labels in the label-list. Then a jump is made to the label pointed to by the number obtained through the evaluation of that s-expression.

Because the cooperation of the compiled state with the rest of the grammar has to be secured, we must save here the remaining positions of labels (in BRANCH function) instead of the remaining texts of arcs (see sec. 4.4) in the function PROCESS_STATE.

The compiler may be written using the recursive descent method. Its purpose is to generate a function for the given state, evaluation of which would be equivalent to the interpretation of that state. For example, the code for the CAT arc may look like the following:

```
ARCi (AND (CATEGORY_SATISFIED? '<category>)
          <arc-test>
          (PROGN (STORE_ATN_CONF '<(i+1  i+2  ...  i+k)>)
               (SETQ ADVANCE? T)
               ((LAMBDA (*)
                   (PROGN  <actions>*))
                 (GET_ROOT_FORM LEX))
               (RETURN T)  ))
```

The entities enclosed in angle brackets are filled in at the time of compilation with the proper elements of the arc texts.

Other arcs are realized similarly with respect to the distinct aims to which they were assigned.

Let us look at the following example. We have an ATN state of the following form:

```
(S/  (PUSH P/ (GETR R1)  (TRANSMIT *)(TO S/1))
     (CAT L1 T (SETR R2 *)(TO S/2))
     (JUMP S/3))
```

The function generated for that state is given below:

```
(S/ (LAMBDA NIL
     (PROG NIL
        (OR ARCS (GO ARC1))
        (BRANCH (ARC1 ARC2 ARC3) (CAR ARCS))
        ARC1 (AND (GETR R1)
                  (PROGN (STORE_ATN_CONF '(2 3))
                     (SETQ ADVANCE? NIL)
                     (STORE_PUSH '((TRANSMIT *)(TO S/1)))
                     (SETQ STATE 'P/)
                     (RETURN T) ))
        ARC2 (AND (CATEGORY_SATISFIED? 'L1) T
                  (PROGN (STORE_ATN_CONF '(3))
                     (SETQ ADVANCE? T)
                     ((LAMBDA (*)
                           (PROGN (SETR R2 *) (TO S/2)))
                        (GET_ROOT_FORM LEX))
                     (RETURN T)  ))
        ARC3 (AND T
                  (PROGN (SETQ ADVANCE? NIL)
                     (TO S/2)
                     (RETURN T) ))    )))
```

The code presented here may be optimized. In the code for the last arc, the storage of the actual configuration is not included because there are no other reamining arcs left to be tried after the backtrack.

5.0 EDITOR

As the last component of the set of programs suitable for writing, testing and debugging ATN grammars, I would like to propose a simple editor.

Such a program should facilitate making changes in the grammar or cre-

ating new ones. Among the most desirable operations are: adding and removing states from a network; adding and deleting arcs in the scope of
a given state; and modifying a particular arc. Editors should be able
to present the state or even the whole subnet in a readable manner as
well.

5.1 Realization

A special file, with direct access, containing every state in the grammar (represented as an s-expression) is created during the first loading
of the grammar. The addresses of states in that file are stored in the
association list with the form

    ((state1 . addr1) (state2 . addr2) ... (staten . addrn))

which is the binding of the atom INDEX. The name of each subnet is bound
to the list of its states.

After compiling a part of the grammar, some ATN states are changed to
corresponding LISP functions which are entirely different from the s-expressions defining these states. Besides, there is no way to obtain any
visual form of any state after it has been compiled to the machine code.
Thus, one cannot modify such parts of the grammar if the original s-expressions defining these fragments of the net are released. In this situation we can easily obtain the required states from the file (mentioned above) and perform any modifications with the use of the editor.

The main purpose of this program is to make modifications in any state
of the grammar. At first, the correct definition of desired state must
be retrieved. If the state was not compiled then its original version
is accessible. No special actions need to be performed. Otherwise, the association list INDEX is searched for the disk address of
the given state, the original definition of which is then read from a
file.

After modifying the state, the necessary changes are made in the whole
system:

1. The new version of the state definition is stored in a new place in
   a file.
2. The new disk address is associated with the state name on the list
   INDEX.

3. The improved state is compiled, if need be.

4. The former version of the compiled state (if it was compiled) is removed from the system.

Using the LISP editor to perform any modifications in the state seems
to be the most appropriate way. This enables the user to perform most
of the acceptable commands of the LISP editor like adding, removing,
changing or finding s-expressions. The possibility of adding paranthes-
es is also a very useful feature.

The set of commands for editing ATN grammars is as follows:

- (EDATN <subnet>)

    <subnet> is the name of a network to be edited. The state contai-
    ning the actual definitions of states is opened. It initializes
    the work of the editor.

- EDIT-S <state-name>

    If the given state <state-name> has been compiled then its actual
    definition is restored.

- ADD-S <subnet-name>

    The system demands the state definition of the user, which, when
    presented, is added to the network <subnet-name>. Surely the state
    will be connected logically with the whole network by the user.

- REM-S <state-name> <subnet-name>

    The state <state-name> is removed from the network <subnet-name>.

- ADD-A n

    The system demands the arc definition which, when presented, is
    added after the n-th arc in the list of arcs of the state being
    edited.

- REP-A n

    The system demands the arc definition which, when presented, is
    substituted for the n-th arc in the state being edited.

- REM-A n

    The n-th arc is removed from the state being edited.

The last commands must be proceeded by the EDIT-S command.

- P-STATE <state-name>

    The system prints the state <state-name>.

- P-ATN <subnet-name>

    The network <subnet-name> is printed.

- FILE

    The performed editions are finished. All modified states remain
    uncompiled. The work of the editor is stopped.

- (FILE COMP)

    All modified states are compiled to LISP functions. The work
    of the editor is finished.

- (FILE COMP COMP)

    All modified states are compiled to machine code. The work of the
    editor is finished.

In this realization the actual form of the grammar is reflected in the
association list INDEX. This allows restoration of all the versions of
the grammar. It may be achieved by stacking subsequent INDEXes.

Creation of entirely new grammars is also possible with the EDATN.

5.2 Example of an Operation

Let us assume that a subnet EXAMPLE is given, (see below).

```
(EXAMPLE
    (S/      (WRD A T (SETR A *) (TO S/1))
             (JUMP S/2))
    (S/1     (WRD B T (SETR B *) (TO S/2))
             (PUSH P/ T (SETR P *) (TO S/P)))
    (S/P     (POP (LIST (GETR A) (GETR B) (GETR C) )))
    (S/2     (POP 'FAIL)) )
```

Assume that we want to add the state s/12, change the arc in state S/2
and add the arc in state S/. The modified states are compiled to LISP
functions.

```
(EDATN EXAMPLE)
>>EDIT-S S/
>>ADD-A 1
GIVE ARC DEFINITION :

(WRD B T (SETR B *) (TO S/12))
>>P-STATE S/
    (S/ (WRD A T (SETR A *) (TO S/1))
        (WRD B T (SETR B *) (TO S/12))
        (JUMP S/2))
>>ADD-S EXAMPLE
GIVE STATE DEFINITION :
(S/12 (WRD A T (SETR A *) (TO S/2)))
>>EDIT-S S/2
>>REP-A 1

GIVE ARC DEFINITION :
(WRD D T (SETR A *) (TO S/P))
>>(FILE COMP)
STATES (S/ S/12 S/2) COMPILED TO LISP CODE
BYE
```

6.0 CONCLUSION

In this paper I have described the implementation of an ATN based on
Earley's algorithm for parsing context-free languages and an example
of implementation of cascaded ATN grammars.

The former is suitable for syntactic grammars, especially those which
contain sentences with many possible parsings.

The latter is a realization of another, more powerful mechanism - cascaded ATN. I have characterized the advantages of this approach to natural language recognition, especially to dividing the process of examining utterances to subparts such as phonology, lexicography, syntactics, and semantics. This method almost immediately achieves the
advantages of the grammar being factored.

In both cases a proposed compiler was described. These implementations
are intended to facilitate the realization of a basic system and to
adapt existing systems to new domains of knowledge.

I would like to extend special thanks to Prof. Leonard Bolc for constant encouragement in writing this paper, and to Arkadiusz Lesniewski and Tomasz Strzalkowski who read the manuscript and suggested many valuable modifications.

7.0 REFERENCES

Aho, A.V., Ullman, J.D. [1972] "The Theory of Parsing Translation and Compiling", Prentice-Hall, Inc., Englewood Cliffs, N.J.

Bates, M. [1978] "The Theory and Practice of Augmented Transition Network Grammars", in Bolc, L. (ed.), "Natural Language Communication with Computers".

Bolc, L. (ed.) [1978] "Natural Language Communication with Computers" in "Lecture Notes in Computer Science" vol. 63, Springer-Verlag.

Bolc, L. et. al. [1980] "The Dialogue - Natural Language Information System", Report of the Institute of Informatics, Warsaw University (in Polish).

Burton, R.R., Woods, W.A. [1976] "A Compiling System for Augmented Transition Networks", presented at the ICCL, Ottawa, Canada.

Cercone, N., Mercer, R. [1980] "Design of Lexicons in Some Natural Language Systems", presented to the Sixth International Symposium of The Association of Literary and Linguistics Computing, Cambridge, England.

Earley, J. [1970] "An Efficient Context-Free Parsing Algorithm", Communication of the ACM. 13, 1970.

Finin, T.W. [1977] "An Interpreter and Compiler for Augmented Transition Networks", Report t-48 Coordinated Science Laboratory, University of Illinois, Urbana, Illinois.

Haraldson, A. [1975] "LISP-details. Interlisp/360-370", Uppsala Universitet.

Moon, D.A. [1974] "Maclisp Reference Manual", Project MAC - M.I.T., Cambridge, MA.

Weinreb, D., Moon, D.A. [1979] "LISP Machine Manual", Artificial Intelligence Laboratory of M.I.T., Cambridge, MA.

Woods, W.A. [1970] "Transition Network Grammars for Natural Language
    Analysis", Communication of the ACM. 13, 1970.

Woods, W.A. et. al. [1976] "Speech Understanding Systems, Final Report
    Vol. IV (Syntacs and Semantics)", BBN Report No. 3438, Bolt
    Beranek and Newman Inc., Cambridge, MA.

Woods, W.A. [1978] "Research in Natural Language Understanding", BBN
    Report No. 3963, Bolt Beranek and Newman Inc., Cambridge, MA.

Woods, W.A. [1980] "Cascaded ATN Grammars", in American Journal of Com-
    putational Linguistics, vol. 6, Number 1.

Symbolic Computation
Managing Editors: **J. Encarnação, P. Hayes**
Artificial Intelligence
Editors: **L. Bolç, A. Bundy, J. Siekmann, A. Sloman**

Automation of Reasoning 1

Classical Papers on Computational Logic 1957-1966
Editors: **J. Siekmann, G. Wrightson**
1983. XII, 525 pages. ISBN 3-540-12043-2

Automation of Reasoning 2

Classical Papers on Computational Logic 1967–1970
Editors: **J. Siekmann, G. Wrightson**
1983. XII, 637 pages. ISBN 3-540-12044-0

Logic has emerged as one of the fundamental disciplines of computer science. Computational logic, which continues the tradition of logic in a new technological setting, has led to such diverse fields of applications as automatic program verification, program synthesis, question answering systems, and deductive data bases as well as logic programming and the 5th generation computer system.
These two volumes, the first covering the years 1957–1966 and the second, 1967–1970, contain those papers which shaped and influenced the field of computational logic. They make available the classical works in the field, which in many cases were difficult to obtain or had not previously appeared in English.

N. J. Nilsson
Principles of Artificial Intelligence

1982. 139 figures. XV, 476 pages. ISBN 3-540-11340-1
(Originally published by
Tioga Publishing Company, 1980)

Contents: Prologue. – Production Systems and AI. – Search Strategies for AI Production Systems. – Search Strategies for Decomposable Production Systems. – The Predicate Calculus in AI. – Resolution Refutation Systems. – Rule-Based Deduction Systems. – Basic Plan-Generating Systems. – Advanced Plan-Generating Systems. – Structured Object Representations. – Prospectus. – Bibliography. – Author Index. – Subject Index.

Springer-Verlag
Berlin
Heidelberg
New York
Tokyo

Lecture Notes in Computer Science

Editors:
G. Goos, J. Hartmanis

Volume 63

Natural Language Communication with Computers

Editor: **L. Bolc**
1978. 45 figures, 3 tables. V, 292 pages
ISBN 3-540-08911-X

Contents: A formalism for the description of question answering systems. – Access to data base systems via natural language. – An overview of Plidis. A problem solving information system with German as query language. – Metamorphosis grammars. – The theory and practice of augmented transition network grammars. – Syntactic analysis of written Polish.

Volume 119
G. Hirst

Anaphora in Natural Language Understanding: A Survey

1981. XIII, 128 pages. ISBN 3-540-10858-0

Contents: Introduction. – Anaphora. – Traditional Approaches to Anaphora. – The Need for Discourse Theme in Anaphora Resolution. – Discourse-Oriented Anaphora Systems and Theories. – Constraints and Defaults in Anaphor Resolution. – The Last Chapter. – References. – Index of Names. – Subject Index.

Volume 138

6th Conference on Automated Deduction

New York, USA, June 7–9, 1982
Editor: **D. W. Loveland**
1982. VII, 389 pages. ISBN 3-540-11558-7

This book contains the papers given at the 6th Conference on Automated Deduction held in June, 1982 at the Courant Institute of Mathematical Sciences New York University. These conferences are the primary international forum for reporting research in all aspects of automated deduction and address such issues as the design and implementation of automated theorem proving systems, experimentation with theorem provers, the capability and efficiency of various representations and control structures for automated deduction, and domains of application for automated deduction.

Springer-Verlag
Berlin
Heidelberg
New York
Tokyo